ACTIVISM
THAT
WORKS

ACTIVISM
THAT
WORKS

edited by
Elizabeth Whitmore,
Maureen G. Wilson
& Avery Calhoun

Fernwood Publishing • Halifax & Winnipeg

Editing: Jessica Antony
Design: Brenda Conroy
Cover design: John van der Woude
Printed and bound in Canada by Hignell Book Printing

Published in Canada by Fernwood Publishing
32 Oceanvista Lane
Black Point, Nova Scotia, B0J 1B0
and 748 Broadway Avenue, Winnipeg, Manitoba, R3G 0X3
www.fernwoodpublishing.ca

Fernwood Publishing Company Limited gratefully acknowledges the financial support of the
Government of Canada through the Canada Book Fund, the Canada Council for the Arts,
the Nova Scotia Department of Tourism and Culture, the Manitoba Department of Culture,
Heritage and Tourism under the Manitoba Publishers Marketing Assistance Program and the
Province of Manitoba, through the Book Publishing Tax Credit, for our publishing program.

Library and Archives Canada Cataloguing in Publication

Whitmore, Elizabeth
Activism that works / Elizabeth Whitmore, Maureen G. Wilson, Avery Calhoun.

Includes bibliographical references and index.
ISBN 978-1-55266-411-7

1. Social justice—Canada. 2. Social action—Canada. 3. Social reformers— Canada. I. Wilson,
Maureen G. (Maureen Grace), 1943- II. Calhoun, Avery, 1959- III. Title.

HM671.W49 2011   303.3'72   C2010-908037-8

CONTENTS

ACKNOWLEDGEMENTS

Social justice activists everywhere inspired us to do this research project and to write this book. As this book goes to press, the importance of effective citizen activism is underscored as we watch the processes and outcomes of uprisings across the Arab world. We want to begin by thanking them for their commitment and tireless efforts in working for a better world.

We are enormously grateful to the nine groups and organizations that participated with us in this research. We have been humbled by their willingness to dedicate time and effort to this project in spite of the enormous demands on them of the very important work that they do every day. They have taught us a great deal. Their considerable wisdom, grounded in the world of practice, has counterbalanced our sometimes limited academic perspectives. Thank you to all those who took the time to share their knowledge in the interviews, workshops and the symposium. Without their insights, this book could not have been written.

A number of research assistants made invaluable contributions to the research. Thank you so very much to Marleny Muñoz, Maria Rasouli, Brenda Ingram, Kate Baillie and Casey Lynn Rosewood. We could not have done this without them. Our appreciation also goes to Jackie Stutt for her incredible speed in transcribing interviews.

We hardly have enough words to express our appreciation to Ann Buxbaum for her indispensible assistance with the symposium and in editing parts of the final manuscript. We also are most grateful to Innovative Development Expertise & Advisory Services (IDEAS) for their very helpful support. Thanks also to Lisa Lorenzetti and Michael Stephens for their marvellous work in facilitating the symposium. And to Rita and Venor Calhoun, who so generously lent us their lovely home by the lake (three times) as a retreat to focus on our writing, we offer a special thank you.

Our sincere appreciation, of course, goes to the Social Sciences and Humanities Research Council (SSHRC) for their financial support of this research.

Finally, thanks Fernwood Publishing for publishing this work. Our thanks go to the helpful comments by the two anonymous reviewers. We especially appreciate Wayne Antony, Beverly Rach, Jessica Antony and Debbie Mathers for their patience and commitment to making this book happen.

FOREWORD

Timing, they say, is everything. Timing and relationships. Timing and re-lationships and heart. Timing and relationships and heart and a strength of vision. I am deeply honoured to have been asked to add a few words to a study which is well timed and needed, is based on deep and on-going relationships by some of Canada's most respected scholar-activists, vibrates with concerns of the heart and is in itself an action, an activist contribution representing a vision for a way forward.

Moving into the second decade of the twenty-first century, scholars, community activists, policy makers and even folks coming from the private sector are taking a new look at the relationship between knowledge, agency, justice, sustainability and the quality of life for all the people in our families, communities, regions, nations and the world. The market utopian dream, what Whitmore, Wilson and Calhoun refer to as market fundamentalism, has continued to hold our societies in its grip. And this is in spite of a decade that has seen a rise of fundamentalist religions, violence and security paranoia unimaginable years ago. Homelessness, which did not exist as a generalized phenomenon in Canada fifteen years ago, is now at the centre of urban concern in all our cities. Funding cuts to our civil society organizations, which began in the mid 1990s, have continued on unabashed as the very fabric of our once heralded social safety net is being shredded by governments at all levels and of all political ideologies. The times remind me of the words of Herman Daly and John Cobb Jr. in their 1989 classic, *The Common Good*, who said,

> at a deep level of our being we find it hard to suppress the cry of anguish, the scream of horror — the wild words required to express wild realities. We human beings are being led to a dead end — all too literally. We are living by an ideology of death and accordingly we are destroying our own humanity and killing the planet. Even the one great success of the program that has governed us, the at-tainment of material affluence, is now giving way to poverty.

The oil sands of Alberta and the oil disaster of our era in the Gulf of Mexico are but two examples of the death of which Daly and Cobb speak.

But while many of the powerful continue to explore how best to sustain a gravy train of personal greed and wealth unseen before in human history, new relationships, new alliances and new strategies are being forged amongst the multiple and diverse actors engaged in knowledge creation and knowledge sharing for enhanced benefits for society. Concepts and structures are emerging from various locations and actors that challenge traditional ideas of who are the knowledge makers, who are the knowledge users. We hear of and read about notions such as social innovation, community-based research, indigenous methodologies, knowledge mobilization, exchange, translation and impact. Community groups are now regularly asked for "evidence-based" strategies for their proposals. What is emerging is a new recognition that knowledge for positive community change is being produced daily in community groups such as the Storytellers' Foundation in rural British Columbia, in the anti-poverty fair trade campaigns of Oxfam, by social workers with a new vision for change not just making do and by those who use drama to both create and share knowledge for change. Critical knowledge for change that builds social capital, community resilience and sustainability exists in the practices of our social movements and our activist groups. An emerging challenge for the engaged scholars of our era is to learn to listen to these voices, to support movements and community energies for change and to form new permanent alliances with the transformative energies of change that continue to give us hope for a different future.

Whitmore, Wilson and Calhoun are leaders of the Canadian movement of engaged scholars who give visibility to social movement knowledge makers, create alliances for the long term with them and begin to break down the fragmented and isolated ways that knowledge has been contained for too long. Along the way, they make the case that listening to social movements also leads to better theory.

Budd Hall
Founding Director, Office of Community Based Research
University of Victoria
Victoria, British Columbia

EDITORS AND CONTRIBUTORS

Editors

Elizabeth Whitmore
Bessa has been (and will continue to be) an activist all of her adult life. A Professor Emerita at Carleton University School of Social Work, her experience includes community organizing and international social development, with a particular interest in participatory action research and evaluation methodologies.

Maureen G. Wilson
Maureen has worked with development projects in several countries and has a special interest in popular responses to the human impacts of globalization. She is currently a professor in the Faculty of Social Work and Co-Chair of the Consortium for Peace Studies at University of Calgary.

Avery Calhoun
Avery's professional experience includes program development, implementation and evaluation in the areas of sexual assault, family violence and restorative justice. She is an associate professor at the University of Calgary.

Contributors

Rod Adachi (Alberta College of Social Workers)
Rod is Alberta born and raised. He holds a Bachelor of Arts from the University of Alberta, a Bachelor of Social Work from the University of Calgary and a Master of Social Work from the University of British Columbia. Rod's social work experience includes practice with disabled children and their families, mental health, home care, community development, diversity training and professional regulation. Rod has been the executive director and registrar for the Alberta College of Social Workers (ACSW) since 1995.

Anne Docherty (The Storytellers' Foundation)
Anne leads projects and campaigns to ensure that the citizens of her region (who are often pushed to the margins) are engaged in building social, cul-

tural and economic assets. Anne does most of this work through her role in Storytellers' Foundation in Hazelton, B.C.

Ryan Geake (Disability Action Hall)

Ryan Geake has a Bachelor of Social Work and Master of Social Work from the University of Calgary. He has worked in the disability sector for over twenty years and feels very fortunate to have stumbled into this work and the Calgary SCOPE Society, where he is currently the Executive Director. He loves working with others who are committed to strengthening the public sector and supporting movements of people who have a vision for a more interesting and fair society.

Colleen Huston (Disability Action Hall)

Colleen has been a member of the Disability Action Hall for the last dozen years. Being part of the Disability Rights Movement has helped build relations with artists, activists, politicians and community. Colleen hopes to be illuminated for years to come by the voices of the disabled community.

Bill Hynd (Oxfam Canada)

Bill has been actively engaged in social justice advocacy for over thirty years, working on many local, national and international campaigns. He has been working with Oxfam Canada for twenty-five years, first as a regional programmer based in St. John's, Newfoundland and then, for the past ten years, as coordinator of national campaigns. Bill is a graduate of Memorial University of Newfoundland.

Sheena Jamieson (Youth Project)

Sheena Jamieson is from Nova Scotia and a graduate of the University of King's College. She has been involved with the Youth Project since 2003 and appreciates all the youth, staff and volunteers who make it a great place to be.

Derek MacCuish (Social Justice Committee)

Derek is Executive Director of the Social Justice Committee (SJC) of Montreal and editor of *Upstream Journal* magazine. He coordinates the SJC's advocacy on global economic policy and institutional reform. From 2000 to 2007 he also taught at Concordia University.

Carol Miller (Oxfam Canada)

Carol has worked twenty years in the field of international development, focusing on women's rights and gender equality issues. She is currently manager of the Monitoring, Evaluation, Learning and Knowledge Sharing Unit at Oxfam Canada. Previous posts include Learning and Accountability Specialist at Oxfam Canada, Gender Policy Analyst with the UK Advocacy Team, ActionAid UK, and Research Associate with the United Nations

Research Institute for Social Development in Geneva. She holds a M.Sc. in politics (London School of Economics) and a D.Phil. in modern history (Oxford University).

Sharon Montgomery (Calgary Raging Grannies)
Sharon Montgomery is a retired teacher who now devotes her life to writing, energy healing and social and political activism. She is the author of "Your Invisible Bodies: A Reference for Children and Adults About Human Energy Fields," and has been published in several magazines and educational journals. Her website is <sharonmontgomery.wordpress.com>.

Maria Rasouli (Research Assistant for the project)
Maria Rasouli earned her PhD in organizational psychology and completed a post-doctoral research fellowship in Eric Sprott School of Business at Carleton University where she teaches courses in "Organizational Behaviour" and "Women in Management". She has over ten years' experience conducting quantitative and qualitative research and her expertise is in the areas of gender, migration and employment, and also program evaluation. In her dissertation, she studied the career adjustment of immigrant women in Canada for which she won the Best Paper Award from the Gender and Diversity Division of the Administrative Sciences Association of Canada in 2008. Dr. Rasouli also conducted research for several program evaluations to evaluate a number of settlement and employment facilitation programs offered to newcomers in Ottawa. Dr. Rasouli's research interests include social justice and diversity in organizations and she continues to work as a research consultant in those fields

Marlo Raynolds (The Pembina Institute)
Senior Advisor to the Pembina Institute, Marlo served as its Executive Director until January 2011. He has worked with the Institute since 1995 in the development and practical application of triple-bottom-line decision-making tools, strategies for sustainability and policy research and advocacy. He holds a PhD in mechanical engineering from the University of Alberta and was recognized as one of Canada's "Top 40 Under 40" for 2008.

Lori Sigurdson (Alberta College of Social Workers)
Lori grew up in a small town in Northern Alberta and then moved to the big city; Edmonton. She has worked as a social worker for over twenty years in various fields of practice: children's services, mental health, community development, advocacy and education. Currently, Lori is Professional Affairs Coordinator for the Alberta College of Social Workers. She has a Bachelor of Arts in political science from the University of Alberta and both a Bachelor and Master of Social Work from the University of Calgary.

Amy Taylor (The Pembina Institute)

One of two economists on staff at the Pembina Institute., Amy has been with the Institute since May of 2000. As Director of the Institute's Public Sector Services Group she is responsible for substantial project development and management, client relations and staff supervision and mentoring.

Leighann Wichman (Youth Project)

Leighann is Executive Director of the Youth Project in Halifax. She has been involved in the organization since joining it in 1993 as a youth member. She is presently completing a Master of Education at Acadia University.

1

MAKING A DIFFERENCE

Elizabeth Whitmore, Maureen G. Wilson and Avery Calhoun

How do we know when we're making a difference? Stories about success from social justice activists demonstrate the complexities that emerge in efforts to answer this question. In the first of the following two stories, an Oxfam Canada staff member describes perceptions of progress on their "Fair Trade in Coffee" campaign. In the second, a member of the Youth Project, a Halifax-based group advocating for the young GLBT community conveys how multi-dimensioned the concept of success can become.

> We were trying to draw attention to the exploitation of poor coffee farmers and the need for the coffee companies to take action. Really there wasn't a lot of awareness — I think probably none — about Fair Trade coffee when we first decided that we would start campaigning on the issue. It must be ten years ago. We told people, "We're doing a public campaign to draw attention to how some of Canada's bigger coffee producers are benefiting from the current situation and are basically running sweat shops without walls." There were different actions that helped promote Fair Trade products across the country, drawing attention to the coffee business and how unsavoury it is. And we would have displays, we did media interviews, we talked to basically whatever group about the whole notion of coffee and the fact that there was this alternative, this Fair Trade coffee. And we started getting people to go into the coffee shops and restaurants and ask for Fair Trade coffee. Of course, we knew full well there wasn't any, but we would say to them, "Well, if you don't have any, you should consider getting it. Why don't you talk to…?" Through this kind of continued, low-level campaigning, now it is almost impossible to go into a store and not find it. And by no means can we take credit for the fact that Loblaws or Dominion now has all these Fair Trade products. But I would like to think that we played a fairly significant role in getting it on the public agenda.

> The youth created this play where there was an alternate world and there were two teenagers, who were straight, who had to go home to their lesbian moms and gay dads and tell them that they were straight. So it was fun and it was funny and it really put a spin on that. And between the acts of that play, [the youth] did monologues about

their own coming out stories, which were really personal for them. They accomplished this in a very topical, interesting way and it was fun and very personal — this play that has so many messages in it, which means a lot more when it's combined with their own experience. So I think the message is stronger. The interesting thing about the play was that it effected change quickly. Whereas my other experiences to do things were long term that don't really produce tangible results right away... and then people were talking, and it didn't take policies or manuals to get people talking and going through the red tape and all this other stuff that we have to do. We just did a play and reached out to people directly and it was good.

This book is about successful activism, as described by activists themselves reflecting on their own work. The activists are from nine diverse groups and organizations across Canada devoted to making a difference in the world by furthering social or environmental justice. We asked eighty-six individual activists from these groups with whom we partnered to talk about what success or effectiveness means to them and what they thought were factors or conditions that contributed to success. The incredible richness and variety of stories they told us constitute the heart of the book. These stories are shared in chapters written by the activists themselves. In the other chapters, we describe the philosophical background, the context, and the methodology of the project and attempt to weave its various parts together in order to make sense of the whole. Our challenge has been to convey the emotions, excitement, and profound commitment the activists express as they reflect on their work.

We approached this project with two primary purposes. First, we wanted to support, in very practical ways, the valuable work of activists. We did this by offering them opportunities to step back and reflect on what they are doing and the effect or impact of their efforts on whether and how they were making a difference. In the often frantic world of activists, such reflection can seem like a luxury. Our second purpose was to explore questions of activist success more broadly in the current political, social and economic context. We hope we've succeeded, in some small way, in accomplishing both our goals.

Words such as "activism" and "advocacy" can evoke different meanings. For our purposes, activism is defined as acting to bring about social, political, economic or environmental change for a more just, sustainable and peaceful world. Activism takes many forms. "Not only resistance and protest should count as activism, but also building relationships between people that foster change in the community" (Hodgson and Brooks 2007: 20). Klugman (2010: 2) defines social justice advocacy as working for

> structural and enduring changes that increase the power of those who are most disadvantaged politically, economically, and socially. It tackles the root and avoidable causes of inequities for those who are systematically and institutionally disadvantaged by their race,

ethnicity, economic status, nationality, gender, gender expression, age, sexual orientation, or religion.

Advocacy can be defined as acting or speaking on behalf of others; it can also mean acting in solidarity with others, or advocating on behalf of one-self or one's own group. Our participating groups and organizations span these definitions. Some focus on advocating on behalf of the general public, others work in solidarity with particular populations while still others are self-advocates. Some involve a combination or even all three.

We came to this project as social researchers who have also been engaged as activists. It was our hope to support the work of activists by bringing to it additional resources in the form of our time and that of our research as-sistants, thanks to a grant from the Social Sciences and Humanities Research Council of Canada (SSHRC).

What we have learned in this project derives from what the activist participants have told us in interviews, workshops, the symposium and in the chapters they have written for this book. The beads on the necklace on the cover of this book, a metaphor brought to us by the Storytellers' Foundation, can be seen as representing the many interconnected individual ideas, thoughts and people coming together to create a story, reflecting the richness and complexity of what activists told us.

This book is divided into three parts. In the first part (Chapters 1 and 2), we discuss the current context surrounding activism and how that context informed our project, particularly its critical and emancipatory dimensions. We summarize how others have assessed activist effectiveness and briefly describe how we worked with the groups and organizations in this project. The set of chapters that comprise Part 2 (Chapters 3 through 10) were contributed by our deliberately diverse[1] selection of activist organizations.[2] Using their own formats and stories, authors representing each group convey what success means in their particular context, the factors or conditions they experience that facilitate success, their hopes and dreams and questions and challenges in relation to their work.

The Oxfam Canada chapter tells us how they organized and mobilized people in the highly effective *Fair Trade in Coffee* campaign. The Disability Action Hall chapter describes how some of the most challenged people in Canadian society have come to see their liberation as bound up with that of others, leading them to begin to shift from seeing themselves as "self-advo-cates" to thinking of themselves as simply "activists." The Alberta College of Social Workers describe their campaign to achieve regulation of the profes-sion and its impact on their mandate for social justice. The Raging Grannies chapter teaches us about strategies that use humour to get across a serious message. The chapter from the Pembina Institute takes us through what they learned in the course of their efforts to help Albertans to understand that they (not the oil companies) are the owners of the oil sands, and to persuade government regulatory agencies that their royalty rates are unfair to those owners. The Halifax-based Youth project, in comic book format, convey the energy and creativity of their efforts to both support GLBT youth and address homophobia in the larger community. The Montreal-based Social Justice Committee shares how they are able to attract and retain their enthusiastic team of volunteers. Finally, the Storytellers' Foundation, based in British Columbia, emphasizes the importance of relationships as fundamental to individual and community change.

The third part of the book consists of two chapters. In Chapter 11, we summarize what we came to understand as the range of meanings of success/effectiveness in activism and how it is facilitated. Finally, in Chapter 12 we provide our own reflections on what we have learned, and introduce complexity science as providing a perspective that may approximate, better than conventional science, what we and our activist colleagues have come to understand about the nonlinear relationships between social change and the efforts of activists.

Notes

1. Because of our motivation to be supportive, if not of some assistance, to these groups, this diversity does not extend to include groups whose objectives we find offensive.
2. Nine activist groups/organizations participated in the project; eight groups accepted the invitation to contribute a book chapter.

2

BUILDING SUCCESS
IN SOCIAL ACTIVISM

Maureen G. Wilson, Elizabeth Whitmore and Avery Calhoun

Social activism can make a difference. And activism that works can generate more activism that works. The neoliberal agenda must be credited
with engendering a strongly felt and remarkably creative set of international
responses to its impacts — not just in rejecting or resisting its policies, but also
in a ferment of activity in generating visions of alternatives. In this chapter
we discuss backgrounds to our work: neoliberal hegemony, its consequences
and contesters; emancipatory social inquiry traditions that inform us; efforts
by others to assess the effectiveness of the work of activists; and finally how
we and our activist collaborators carried out this project.

Neoliberalism and Its Discontents

Social activism is currently situated in the dual realities of the continuing
ascendancy of neoliberal policies on one hand and the growing importance
of the role of citizen groups in opposing them on the other. Farmer/phil-
osopher Nettie Wiebe (1998), speaking of a visit to her ancestral village in
Europe, described the marketplace in the town square as being "hemmed
in" by buildings of public purpose. This is exactly the reverse, she noted, of
what occurs with neoliberal rules, under which the market is given preced-
ence over public purpose. Neoliberalism, an ideology that makes the market
central in governing economic, social and political life, is girded by a belief
in the inherent wisdom of the market, assuming that the rules of the market
should govern societies, rather than the other way around.

Voices opposing this market fundamentalism point out that promoting
competition between individuals, businesses and nations logically results in
a diminishing minority of fortunate winners and an overwhelming global

majority who are the losers. The processes of neoliberal globalization have been accompanied by degradation of social, political, economic and environmental conditions for the vast majority of the world's population.

The Impacts

For Economic and Social Justice

The implementation of the neoliberal global agenda has been accompanied by growing disparities between rich and poor, both within and between countries (UN 2010, ILO 2008). The United Nations Development Program has long decried the "inequitable effects of globalization driven by markets and profit… a grotesque and dangerous polarization between people and countries benefiting from the system and those that are merely passive recipients of its effects" (UNDP 1997: 1). Unfortunately, the years since 1997 have seen little progress (Finn 2010). In 2008, the International Labour Organization's *World of Work Report* concluded that the worldwide gap between richer and poorer households has continued to widen, and that "financial globalization — caused by deregulation of international capital flows — has been a major driver of income inequality" (ILO 2008: 2).[1] With 43 percent of the global workforce earning less than $2 per day, the number of people going hungry is increasing. In September 2008, CARE International reported that "[in the past two years] another 100 million people have been pushed into hunger and can no longer afford food" (CARE 2008: 1).

Recent decades, then, have been a development disaster for many of the world's poorest countries.[2] As a consequence of neoliberal globalization, ordinary people world-wide are dislocated and thrown out of work, needed social programs are dismantled and a very few people become very rich. The realities associated with the dramatic economic crash of 2008 that so traumatized the privileged had long since been the companion of the global majority. Yet while the 1.3 billion people living in the world's poorest countries lived on an average annual income of $573, following the 2008 financial crisis, $15 trillion in public funds was used to bail out private banks. $15 trillion is approximately one fourth of the world's total income (Ransom 2009).

For the Environment

There is mounting evidence of the disproportionate impact of negative effects of climate change on the world's poor (UNDP 2007/2008), effects that were exacerbated by the 2008 financial crisis. "Just as the market has proved incapable of controlling the dangerous excesses of international finance, it is failing to reduce greenhouse gas emissions, or to kick-start the dramatic shift towards zero-carbon economies we so desperately need" (Worth 2009b: 11). The increasing economic and political power of businesses and investors in recent decades, strengthened immensely by globalization (Stanford

2008), has produced an increasing concern that inequalities in wealth and power are fueling the global climate crisis (Worth 2009b, Nikiforuk 2008). The production of greenhouse gases continues to rise in the richest countries, while the poorest of the poor are disproportionately affected through increasingly frequent "natural" disasters including flooding, droughts and other extreme weather events, with attendant crop failures, rising world food prices, malaria, malnutrition and diarrhea (NI 2009). Thus there is an additional sense in which "the rich world owes the poor world an ecological debt" (Worth 2009a: 8).

Threats to Democracy and National Sovereignty

"Free" trade agreements, constraining governments to act in accordance with commercial considerations — at the expense of the interests of their own citizens or the environment — are considered by many to represent threats to democracy and to national sovereignty. It is argued that trade agreements giving corporations the power to sue governments, should laws or regulations interfere with commerce, result in the concentration of economic and political power in the hands of corporate elites. This expansion of "rights" and "freedoms" for corporations, with the dismantling of trade and investment barriers, is seen as having disempowered people and governments and transferred power into the hands of global corporations (Korten 2009).[3] In other words, the free trade agreements that allow the interests of corporations to trump those of governments, and the structural adjustment policies associated with globalism, have the effect of reducing the capacity — and right — of governments to protect their citizens from these impacts (Klein 2007).

The Responses

Critiques of Market Fundamentalism

Critiques of market fundamentalism are not new. Polanyi's (1944) historical research demonstrated that national markets are not "natural" but depend on the creation and maintenance of a complicated infrastructure of laws and institutions. As Galbraith notes, markets in this doctrine are "theologically sacrosanct... yet clearly the speculative episode, with increases provoking increases, is within the market itself. And so is the culminating crash" (1993: 106–107). Similarly, Kozul-Wright and Rayment declare, "It is a dangerous delusion to think of the global economy as some sort of 'natural' system with a logic of its own: it is, and always has been, the outcome of a complex interplay of economic and political relations" (2004: 3–4).

There is also unease related to a perception that the diffusion of ideas tends to be one way — from the centres of power outward — with views on democracy and human rights and, perhaps more importantly, the promotion of an "intellectual blueprint... based on a belief about the virtues of markets and private ownership" (Przeworski et al. 1995: viii). In other words, around the question of ideological hegemony.

Challenges to neoliberalism have come not just from intellectuals, but also from within corporate and political elites. By the beginning of the twenty-first century, as economic, social, environmental and political crises proliferated throughout the world, increasing numbers of people at the "centre" had been questioning the wisdom of the neoliberal "miracle" (Soros 1998). Important corporate and political figures were calling for reform, or at least for some kind of supervision of capital. In a May 1999 speech, then World Bank chief economist Joseph Stiglitz criticized the single-minded preoccupation with inflation that resulted in macroeconomic policies stifling growth. There were "signs… of a growing fissure between the IMF's thinking and that of its sister organization, the World Bank" (Elliot 1999: 14). The same year, Canadian Finance Minister Paul Martin stated that, "simply put, in an institutional and legal vacuum, private markets cannot serve social interests, nor can they serve economic interests" (Martin 1999). The Tobin Tax, Nobel Prize-winning economist James Tobin's proposal for a punitive tax on short-run speculative financial transactions, was just one of a number of initiatives being proposed to rein in out-of-control capital.

The 2008 global market collapse brought home the critical importance of these issues, seeming to create overnight neo-Keynesians in corporate circles, with a recognition of the need for re-regulation in the interest of capital accumulation (Martinez 2009).

> Keynes's great contribution was to save capitalism from the capital-ists: if they had had their way, they would have imposed policies that weakened the economy and undermined political support for capitalism. The regulations and reform adopted in the aftermath of the Great Depression worked. Capitalism took on a more human face, and market economies became more stable. But these lessons were forgotten… Keynes's insights are needed now if we're to save capitalism once again from the capitalists. (Stiglitz 2010: 18)

From Governments
Generally speaking, national governments have been spectacularly inef-fective in either challenging the neoliberal global agenda, or in protecting their citizens from its impacts. For poor nations, the tying of their loans to structural adjustment requirements impeded any challenge to these policies. The leadership of most rich nations, on the other hand, has largely bought into the "common sense" of growth/trickle-down economics and the neo-liberal axiom of "bad state/good market" (McMichael 2010: 3). Whether for reasons of ideological complicity with the forces of neoliberalism, or of constraints imposed by international financial institutions or trade agree-

ments, leadership from national governments has thus been little in evidence in addressing issues of social and environmental justice.

In the face of this vacuum, citizen organizations worldwide have been moving into the breach, confronting the threats of corporate globalization to democracy, economic justice, the environment and protection of the commons.

Counterhegemonic Popular Responses

Responses to market-worshipping neoliberalism are perhaps best summed up in the "one no, many yeses" slogan of the World Social Forum (WSF). Meeting in various places around the world, initially as a counterpoint to the annual World Economic Forum in Davos, Switzerland, the WSF represents a broad-based civil society rejection of the neoliberal global agenda (the "no"[4]) and an affirmation of the multiplicity of alternatives generated through the creative genius of ordinary people (the "yeses").

Since the early 1980s, movements in the global South — with consciousness no doubt enhanced by hundreds of years of anti-colonial struggles — have challenged structural adjustment programs, their externally-generated debt burdens, privatizations of publicly owned resources and services, externally funded megaprojects and their attendant debt, the destruction of traditional economies and food security and environmental degradation. In the North, by the middle of the same decade, resistance was mobilizing to proposed free trade agreements that would make the interests of international corporations superior those of governments, allowing corporations to sue governments for any labour, social or environmental protections that might interfere with commercial interests (Wilson and Whitmore 2000).

The emergence of the World Social Forum and other alliances reflects the convergence of circumstances between the dispossessed of the North and the South — a globalized impoverishment in terms of economic and social justice, political power and ideological hegemony — and a resulting attempt at organized resistance, or globalization from below. People have organized sectorally, around specific economic, social, democracy and environment-related issues, and in local, national or cross-national coalitions. Thus, for example, La Via Campesina, an international movement of peasants, small- and medium-sized producers, landless, rural women, indigenous people, rural youth and agricultural workers, was formed to

> develop solidarity and unity among small farmer organizations in order to promote gender parity and social justice in fair economic relations; the preservation of land, water, seeds and other natural resources; food sovereignty; sustainable agricultural production based on small and medium-sized producers. (Via Campesina 2009; Desmarais 2007)

Similarly, in Canada and abroad, organized labour, women's groups, faith groups, indigenous peoples, seniors' and student groups have organized around social, civil and economic rights, anti-poverty and other issues, attempting in their own ways to confront the consequences of the neoliberal agenda — as the potential "other superpower" (Schell 2003).

This new context requires a profound rethinking not just of strategies to confront new kinds, scales and faces of hegemonic power, but of visions of the global "good life" and of democratic ways to advance, enact, sustain and transform them. Where and what are the sources for such a rethinking? A growing number of theorists point to the existence of emergent alternatives grounded in the practices of social movements and the knowledges arising from them (Conway 2004: 12).

Emancipatory Social Inquiry

As Karl Marx famously observed, "the philosophers have only interpreted the world, in various ways; the point, however, is to change it" (Marx 1845: XI).

The unmasking of the social relations of capitalism and their consequences was, in Marx's view, a catalyst needed to bring about this change. A part of this is unmasking how the social relations of capitalism "provide a persuasive basis for liberal freedoms and formal equalities while enabling a dominant class to appropriate the surplus produced by subordinates" (Carroll 2006: 235). These insights and those of social analysts who came after Marx, in particular Antonio Gramsci and Paulo Freire, provide useful points of departure in understanding resistance movements, and in guiding social researchers and practitioners in their relation to them.

Gramsci

Antonio Gramsci made several important advances over classical Marxist theory, developing a body of work which has been widely influential. Gramsci, born in 1891 to a southern Italian peasant family, organized workers' groups as bases for revolution and was imprisoned for these efforts in 1926 by Mussolini. During the eleven years between his imprisonment and his death in jail in 1937, Gramsci developed advances in Marxist thought that have had a wide impact in social and political thought.

The Organic Intellectual

Gramsci (1976) rejected the view that intellectuals were needed to bring theory and ideology (and often leadership) to the masses.[5] Gramsci argued that the working class, like the bourgeoisie before it, is capable of developing from within its ranks its own "organic intellectuals." He believed organic intellectuals, at once ordinary workers and leaders, could be assisted to lead the working class toward hegemony.[6]

Structure and Conjuncture

> Men [sic] make their own history, but… they do not make it under
> circumstances of their own choosing. (Marx 1852)

Gramsci assisted us in thinking about the practicalities of this by distinguishing between "structural" and "conjunctural" analysis. He observed that some
aspects of the social structure are more fundamental and comparatively
permanent (structural), while others are more temporary (conjunctural).
Structural analysis identifies the main power relationships and competing
social and economic interests that make up the structure of our society in
the longer term. (It shows us, for example, that Canada is an industrialized
capitalist country in which the economy is driven primarily by market forces
— with some state intervention — with a dependency relationship with the
U.S. and in which only a minority of the workforce is unionized.) Structural
analysis provides us with a critical base for understanding and action, and
helps us to understand that, as McNally (2002) and organizers of the World
Social Forum put it, "another world is possible."

Conjunctural analysis, as an indispensable partner to this, pertains more
directly to our day-to-day work. It examines the balance of forces and events
in a given moment (conjuncture) for opportunities or constraints to action
at a given point in time, helping us to plan more effective action toward our
shorter-term goals. (For example, "Who are the key actors on this issue?
Who's with us and who's against us? Are there alliances we can form? How
might the financial crisis or the upcoming election affect our opportunities
for action?") The combination of structural and conjunctural analysis, then,
incorporates a means of analysis of broad social forces, a way of clarifying
one's own identity and interests within these, a visioning of desired alternatives and a mechanism for evaluating the current moment in terms of opportunities to act.

Ideological Hegemony

Gramsci affirmed that economic, ideological and political forces must all be
taken into account in achieving social transformation. Distinguishing between
a "War of Position" (a struggle for ideological domination, a war of ideas)
and a "War of Manoeuvre" (armed struggle), he believed it was necessary in
the first instance to win the war of ideas in order to gain the popular support
needed for socialist transformation. The concept of ideological hegemony
refers to the how the ideas of the dominant class — the dominant ideas of
a society — are internalized to the extent that people willingly submit to
their domination and exploitation. These relationships of domination and
exploitation are so embedded in the dominant ideas of a society that the
ideas of the ruling class come to be seen as normal, universal, "common

sense" knowledge.[7] Thus, for example, a pattern of social/economic relations among people (such as free market capitalism) becomes, in people's minds, a natural or inevitable thing, outside of human control.

As Susan George (1997) has reminded us, in recent decades the political right has taken Gramsci's insights on the war of ideas more to heart than have progressive forces. Their understanding of its significance is reflected, for example, in their handsome funding of sympathetic think tanks, through their control of mass media and in their influence in education systems. Groups attempting to challenge the hegemony of the currently dominant ideas of neoliberalism, on the other hand, typically work with very scarce resources. The skills of social analysis, and the understanding that ordinary people are capable of this and of leadership in challenging neoliberal hegemony, are then critical in this contest.

Freire

Brazilian educator Paulo Freire's advocacy of popular education as an option for the poor emerged out of his work in literacy training in the 1960s, based in the Gramscian notion of the organic intellectual. Freire (1970) observed that education systems are not neutral: they usually serve the interests of those in power. Popular education, or education for critical consciousness, involves a participatory process that helps develop people's critical thought, creative expression, and collective action. Freire's ideas and methods quickly attracted attention among Latin American social practitioners and activists. The influence of this thought quickly spread from there to other poor countries, and finally to some parts of the "developed world." Three of Freire's ideas in particular have represented important contributions to activist/social change theory and practice.

Conscientization

Conventional teaching assumes that "knowledge is a gift bestowed by those who consider themselves knowledgeable upon those whom they consider to know nothing" (Freire 1970: 58). Freire contrasts this with a "problem-posing" approach, in which people are viewed as conscious beings, capable of critical reflection. The result is a "dialogic" approach where critical co-investigators dialogue with one another, exploring an issue and drawing on their everyday experience to understand and take a critical stance toward what they have always assumed to be true. Both are assumed to be actors (subjects) in the world, capable of intervening actively and creatively to change it. With this, we have what Freire calls *conscientização* (education for critical consciousness) — the development, through dialogue, of awareness of one's reality and engaging in critical thinking about it as process, as transformation, rather than as something static and unchangeable.

Praxis

Following from Marx's dialectical conception of "praxis" as "the coincidence of the changing of circumstances and of human activity" (Marx 1845), Freire uses the language of action and reflection — a continuous processes of thinking clearly and thoroughly about one's reality, and then acting to change it. Reflection without action he calls "verbalism," idle chatter; action without reflection is "activism," action for action's sake without thought. It is the interaction between the two that is crucial to dialogue and transformation (Freire 1970).[8]

Participatory Action Research

Freire's work has been pivotal in establishing the philosophical foundations of participatory action research. His assumption that ordinary people are capable of generating valid knowledge challenged the view that only experts can create genuine knowledge. This was in part a reaction to conventional positivist models of inquiry that he saw as exploitive and irrelevant to the realities of life for ordinary people. Participatory action research, as conceived by Freire, democratizes the relations among researchers and the researched, privileging participant groups or communities over researchers in terms of control of the research processes and products. Its work is framed explicitly within a context of power and transformation (Hall 1992), with the intention "to produce an analysis in the interest of those about whom knowledge is being constructed" (Campbell and Gregor 2002: 68).

Political Activist Ethnography

"For Marx... the working class was not only the source of social transformation, it provided a perspective internal to capitalism from which to uncover capital's secrets" (Carroll 2006: 235). Institutional ethnographers, believing, along with Marx, in the power of revealed truth as a catalyst for change, attempt to "to explicate the actual social processes and practices organizing people's everyday experience... a sociology in which we do not transform people into objects but preserve their presence as subjects" (Smith 1986: 6).

Building on institutional ethnography to define what he called "political activist ethnography," the late gay activist/researcher George Smith (2006) contributed to the field of activist research by elaborating a "reflexive-materialist research method" to create knowledge in the service of social transformation. His research is "reflexively organized within a materialist understanding of a world that is put together in people's practices and activities" (G. Smith 2006: 53). Much as Mann (1977) noted the clarity with which exploitative social relations can been seen by workers with the rupture of consciousness occurring in the experience of a strike, Smith saw how from the standpoint of an activist in confrontation with authority, a moment of breach when an institution feels challenged is an opportunity to gain insight into both how it operates and its mechanisms of control. The assumption in this research strategy is that, through confrontation with ruling regimes and institutions, researcher/activists can uncover aspects of how they work, and thus develop more effective strategies to create change.

Activists and Researchers

> The test for whether or not research has been successful is the extent to which it enables people to transform the world. (Frampton et al. 2006: 3)

In our view, social inquiry and practice are both at their best when grounded in praxis, "developed out of a dialogue between activism and reflection — practice and theory" (Carroll 2006: 234). This combines the unmasking of the intersecting workings of capitalism, sexism, racism, ableism, ageism, heterosexism and other sources of marginalization and exploitation[9] with action to bring about social transformation.

The insights of Gramsci, Freire and George Smith, among others, make important contributions to emancipatory social inquiry, which can legitimately take a variety of forms. One way of classifying these might be in terms of the identity/positionality of the investigators as *for*, *with*, or *of* the activist groups. The research discussed here can be described as having encompassed, at various times, all three. In doing this, as we describe below, we have employed a process intended to make the groups partners in the research and in the construction of their own knowledge.

Assessing Effectiveness in Creating Social Change

But how do we know, and how can activists know, whether and how they are making a difference in their work? In the past decade there has been an explosion of interest in this area, reflected both in academic and professional literatures, as well as websites of activist organizations and funding agencies alike.[10] For decades prior to this, discussions of evaluation had tended to focus on unidirectional questions of the influence of evaluation studies on policy makers (Mark and Henry 2004) and on attitudes and actions (Henry and Mark 2003). Coffman (2009: 3) notes that

> advocacy has long been considered "too hard to measure"... but this is now changing. Interest in advocacy evaluation is surging and cutting edge advocates are embracing evaluation as a critical part of their work. The main barrier preventing more organizations from using evaluation is a lack of familiarity with how to think about and design evaluations for advocacy efforts that are useful, manageable and resource-efficient.

For Coffman, then, the issue has thus become more *how to* than *whether*. At the same time, the question of *whether* continues to spark lively debate through discussion of the role of values and social justice in evaluation (Freeman 2010; Greene 2001; House and Howe 1999).

In the area of establishing effectiveness, much of the activism evaluation debate centres around two main purposes and consequent methodologies. One focuses on summative accountability (assessing success after the fact), using primarily quantitative methodologies that assume the ability to determine cause and effect. There is increasing agreement, however, that strictly quantitative, summative evaluations are not appropriate for most purposes because they are unable to probe the complexities of the change process.[11] The other directs attention to learning and improving practice, which tends to lead to more mixed method, flexible and complex approaches (Greene 2007; Greene 2010b). Patton, for example, focuses on learning in complex contexts and advocates developmental evaluation (2010: 330–32).

Not surprisingly, those on the front lines of social change have given considerable attention to the question of whether they are making a difference and how they might actually know it.[12] One outcome of these endeavours has been the development of a variety of resources that activist groups can draw from when considering evaluation. Some of these are included in the Resources section at the end of this book.[13]

Principles, Components and Challenges

While there is no consensus on a "right" approach to assessing one's effectiveness, there is a great deal of discussion about principles, components and challenges in doing this work. Several sets of principles have been proposed that can be useful guides, including "expand beyond policy work" (Guthrie et al. 2005: 13) and "let the story be told (add narrative components)" (Egbert and Hoechstetter 2007: 20).[14] There is growing recognition that, what might appear to be a failure, such as no new legislation is passed, may have other positive effects such as the excitement and commitment generated for people not normally involved (Coffman 2007: 3).

Components generally recognized as critical to effective advocacy work relate to reflection, organizational capacity and relationships. In what Chambers (2005: 175) calls a "culture of over-commitment," building in time for reflection is increasingly acknowledged as key to effectiveness (Bagnell Stuart 2007; Chapman, Pereira Jr. and Miller 2006; Chapman and Wameyo 2001; Guthrie et al. 2005; Patton 2010; Reilly 2007; Ringsing and Leeuwis 2008). During planned periods of reflection, informal information is purposefully discussed, and where valid, integrated into organizational practices.

Capacity building and organizational learning, though identified as vital, tend to be "shunted aside in the hectic, day to day tumult of advocacy work" (Raynor, York and Sim 2009: 8–9). Yet, as Raynor, York and Sim conclude, "strong organizational capacity has the potential to be a reliable predictor of successful advocacy outcomes." Many smaller organizations, struggling with limited resources, will have to find efficient ways to evaluate their own effectiveness (Coffman January 2009). Building flexibility into this process is essential, given the constantly shifting nature of activities and desired outcomes (Coffman 2007).

Building relationships and networks among activists and organizations and with decision makers can consolidate efforts and increase effectiveness. This requires a focus on contribution (rather than attribution, as demanded by many funders), an issue with which many activist organizations struggle.

The State of the Art

To date, much of the development of advocacy evaluation has been driven by funders' requirements rather than by activists themselves. "There is clearly a need for greater involvement in this debate by advocacy organizations to ensure their needs are met by any evaluation process" (Whalen 2008: 2). The challenge is "how best to align evaluation practice with real-world advocacy work" (Riesman, Gienapp and Stachowiak 2007: 2). What has been identified as missing?

- Substantially absent from advocacy evaluation is the voice of the advocates themselves (The Innovation Network: 2008).
- Identifying outcomes broader than policy change may help develop ideas of effectiveness in social justice advocacy. Most advocacy/activism evaluation currently focuses on policy change, which Guthrie et al. (2005: 17) describe as "too narrow" because it overlooks "the work building up to policy change and the implementation of policy once passed." Other authors share the belief expressed by Guthrie et al. that effectiveness has been too restrictively defined in the advocacy field (Coffman 2007; Miller 1994; Miller 2004).
- Connecting what activists already know to wider strategic theory about activism and advocacy is a critical need. According to Whalen (2008: 7), "making these connections would take the evaluation beyond a simple catalogue of outcome measures into a strategic review that can drive future planning." He calls for "efforts to link the perceptions and knowledge of participants to wider strategic and policy process theory" (Whalen 2008: 6–7), including activist theory (Alinsky 1969; Moyer 2001; Rose 2005; Stachowiak 2009) that provides essential strategic insights into the reality of political processes and how they can be manipulated.[15]
- In dominant discourses, program logic models are considered essential to "good" evaluation. These models specify the changes activists expect to result from their activities. Some authors have acknowledged that change in complex contexts is difficult to model using these tools,

but nevertheless believe that it can be done (Guijt 2008; Patton 2010; Zimmerman 2000). However, others see the social justice advocacy field as too complex for simple cause-effect models.

These are the elements of the context, then, that has informed the formulation of our own processes for this project.

What We Did

Action research paved the way for our partners to be genuine collaborators in the research and in the construction of their own knowledge. Appreciative inquiry helped focus the activists' reflections on what was already working within their organizations and on preferred future outcomes, which energized their engagement in the project.

Action Research

Action research is described in detail elsewhere (Cooke and Cox 2005; Dick 2004, 2006; Greenwood and Levin 2007; Pyrch 1998; Reason and Bradbury 2001, 2006). Collaboration and dialogue among partners and on practical applications are core aspects of action research (Brown et al. 2003; Brydon-Miller, Greenwood and Maguire 2003; Dick 2007; Greenwood 2007; Gustavsen 2007). It emphasizes the importance of critical reflection based on the premise that rich learning can develop from unpredicted events or outcomes of the research process (Beukema and Valkenburg 2007; Reason and Bradbury 2007). In our project, the workshops and the symposium offered good opportunities for collective reflection (discussed in more detail below).

Appreciative Inquiry

Appreciative inquiry (AI) builds knowledge through a continuous process of inquiry and change, which occur simultaneously as a kind of intervention. It makes use of narrative to draw out success stories, to identify key elements for success, and to build on these.[16] The narrative, or story, is evoked initially by using positive questions that guide the conversation. Although there are several variations, the process of AI generally includes four phases: discovery, dream, design and destiny.[17] The appreciative process engages people in storytelling and captures nuances, emotions and energy that can be missed by other data collection strategies (Bushe 1998; Cooperrider, Whitney and Stavros 2003; Robinson-Easley 1998).

AI, extensively discussed elsewhere (Cooperrider, Barrett and Srivasta 1995; Cooperrider, Whitney and Stavros 2003; Cooperrider and Whitney 2005; Elliot 1999; Zandee and Cooperrider 2008), developed as a complement to conventional forms of action research, taking a more collaborative and participative stance (Dick 2004; Dick 2006). Like action research, appreciative inquiry has become increasingly prominent in the evaluation field (Patton 2003; Patton 2010; Preskill and Catsambas 2006; Preskill and Coghlan 2003). In the context of assessing effective activism, AI seemed an excellent fit for our work.

By definition, AI focuses on the positive or on what has been successful. It shifts the focus from problem-oriented thinking to a process that examines and builds on positive experiences and successes in planning for, designing and implementing future actions. This process informs both our understanding of a situation (theory) and what we do about it (practice). The assumption is that something works in every organization. Evoking and scrutinizing previous positive experiences contributes to future creativity and positive outcomes. The focus is on the process — dialogue, inclusion and collabora-tion. The flexibility of the approach meant we could adapt it to fit our needs and circumstances while still being consistent with its main principles.

Because AI produces narrative data, activists could relate their experi-ences of success as richly detailed stories. People are engaged by telling stories, conveying the details, tones and subtleties typically missed in quan-titative measurement (Bushe 1998; Cooperrider, Whitney and Stavros 2003; Robinson-Easley 1998). Stories are elicited by positive questions that guide the conversation and nurture the participant's engagement. Questions can then be reworded to focus the attention on the most life-giving, life-sustaining stories and elements of whatever phenomena are being explored (Ludema et al. 2001).

Engaging Activist Participants

We wanted to work with a broad range of groups and organizations in order to achieve a mixture of experiences that we would not likely achieve with a more homogeneous group (Brinkerhoff 2003). Through several networks, we issued an invitation to activist groups interested in exploring with us the question, "how do you know when you're making a difference?"[18] From the responses to this invitation, and by reaching out through our own networks, a deliberately diverse selection of activist groups (in terms of themes of focus, organizational size and complexity, demographics, support base, funding and geography) was identified to partner with us in this project. The participating activists ranged from small, local groups to large, national organizations. Each had a different focus of activities. Some are complex, with many staff, others are small, with a handful of staff members, while one has no staff, budget or organizational structure at all. Most depend a great deal on volunteers. The majority receive at least some government funding, though one has no funding (Raging Grannies) and another depends substantially on ongoing church support and donations (Social Justice Committee). Several have existed for many years and others were relatively new. The demographic characteristics of staff members and volunteers range across diverse ages, sexual orientations, abilities, ethnic backgrounds and social class.

The Process

While our approach varied with each of the nine groups, depending on the needs and capacities of both the group and the research team, the process generally involved an introductory workshop for the group, followed by in-depth individual interviews with group members, with appreciative framing of the questions. Following the transcription of the interviews for a particular group, a preliminary thematic analysis of the interviews formed the basis for a second workshop, facilitated by the researchers, to assist the group in clarifying its dreams and moving to the creation of shared vision, action and reflection. Additional workshops followed up on this work to allow the groups to further use what we had learned to enhance their effectiveness. A total of eighty-six activists were interviewed, with a range of five to fifteen interviews per organization. Assuming that most groups would have time and financial constraints, we built in funding for each to hire a research assistant to manage logistics and liaison with us.

The individual interviews were semi-structured, allowing for interviewer-participant probing and dialogue. The interview guide included the following guiding questions:

- Can you tell us a story about a successful project/campaign/social action you have experienced in your work (with the organization or in another context)?
- When is this group at its best? Can you tell us about a time like that?
- What does success look like for your group/organization? What are you most proud of?
  - What conditions were in place that helped make [that project] successful?
- Can you talk about a time when your group/organization successfully overcame an obstacle or challenge?
  - What made that possible?
- Imagine that you fall asleep for five years. When you wake up, what would you hope to see in your group/organization? How is it working? What makes you feel proud? What are some of the things that enabled your organization to succeed?

After the workshops and interviews were complete, we held a two-day symposium for all groups able to attend. The purpose of the symposium was to present the preliminary results, offer space for groups to talk about their experiences and results, and refine our understandings of the meanings of success and factors that contribute to them. Groups had opportunities to network with each other, sharing stories of success in formats of their choice, which allowed for some especially engaging presentations. For example, the

Disability Action Hall, dedicated to collective principles, brought seventeen members to present their stories. Their presentation opened the symposium and set a positive tone of excitement and collaboration. The Youth Project, from Halifax, told their story through a lively, humourous comic book. The Raging Grannies sang a witty song they had written for the symposium. The discussions were full of good energy, lots of laughter and active exchanges of insights as we grappled with ideas about success and how to put it all together. An appreciative spirit infused these conversations, as participants focused attention on what works and why. The following morning, we met to discuss with groups how we would all participate in the production of this book, sharing what we learned and what the book might be called.

Data Analysis: Making Sense of What We Heard

Our analysis of what was told to us in the individual interviews[19] involved an iterative process of coding and categorizing the data and building a set of categories, moving back and forth between the data and our codes and categories until we were satisfied that they reflected what people said. At the broadest level, our codes reflected the two main research questions: how do activists know when their work is successful and what do activists think contributes to their success? Within each of these two main questions, multiple categories, sub-categories and, sometimes, sub-sub-categories were developed as we tried to both honour the differences and respect the similarities in the stories our participants were telling us.

Reflecting on the Process

Dialogue, collaboration, practical application, critical reflection, mutuality and trust are defining characteristics of action research methods such as AI. We tried to be sensitive to all of these throughout our work together. We made efforts to build dialogue and mutuality into every aspect of our collaboration. There were two key aspects that made this process work for our partners. One was timing: it needed to be a time when their needs/interests, at a particular moment, coincided with our research interests. For example, one organization needed to restructure their board of directors and welcomed the opportunity to step back and reflect on the situation. Another was facing a funding crisis. Still another looked for something quite different — they wanted immediate feedback from external stakeholders about their role in what was generally regarded as a successful change effort.

Not only were the activists invited to engage in critical reflection of their work, we, as researchers, also used the ongoing interaction with them and with each other to step back and reflect on what we were doing, how we were doing it and what our results seemed to be saying. We found that taking the time to develop trusting relationships with our partners helped us to make optimal use of visits that were short and spread out over time. The decisive factor in the activists' participation, however, was the potential usefulness of our process and findings for their work.

Notes

1. Neoliberal globalization may have helped to reduce poverty in some of the largest and strongest economies — China and India, for example (UN 2009). However, in comprehensive analyses, "the one point of agreement among all studies is that the level of global inequality is very high" (Anand and Segal 2009: 54).
2. According to Fukuda-Parr and Stewart, "key indicators of human development not only failed to progress but began to register reversals" (2009: 2).
3. Yet, as Korten has commented, "even CEOs are extremely limited by the imperatives of global competition from acting socially responsibly. When they do, they are quickly replaced. When they do not, they are rewarded greatly" (IFG 1996:12).
4. Or the *¡Ya basta!* ("Enough is enough!") of Mexico's Zapatistas.
5. Gramsci advanced beyond the Leninist view that socialist consciousness needed to be brought to the working class from outside by the revolutionary party, through the fusing together of former workers and intellectuals of bourgeois origin. For Gramsci, the role of the political party is to channel the activity of these organic intellectuals and to provide a link between these and certain sections of the traditional intelligentsia. It should be noted that Lenin's own views shifted from this 1902 *What is To Be Done?* perspective to his famous 1919 *"All power to the soviets!"* speech (Lenin 1961).
6. Gramsci believed that through their assumption of conscious responsibility, and with assistance from the more advanced intellectuals of bourgeois origin, the proletariat can advance toward hegemony.
7. Lukács (1971) further developed this with his concept of reification, a process through which an idea comes to be treated as an objective "thing" — the abstraction of relationships and processes into ideological objects of thought.
8. For elaboration on this, see Freire (1970), Chapter III.
9. This requires the courage and intellectual honesty to carry out "a ruthless criticism of everything existing, ruthless in two senses: the criticism must not be afraid of its own conclusions, nor of conflict with the powers that be" (Marx 1978: 13).
10. A number of foundations have acknowledged the legitimacy of social justice advocacy as a strategy for the non-profit sector, and have supported the production of research and materials in this area (Masers 2009; Ranghelli 2009; Reisman, Gienapp and Stachowiak 2007).
11. Refer to, for example, Alliance for Justice 2005; Chapman 2002; Chapman and Wameyo 2001; Coates and David 2002; Coffman 2009; Earl, Carden and Smutylo 2001; Evaluation Exchange 2007; Guthrie et al. 2005; Kellogg Foundation 2007; Kelly 2002; Patton 2010; Reilly 2007; Reisman, Gienapp and Stachowiak 2007; Torjman 1999; Whalen 2008; Wilson-Grau and Nuñez 2007; Woodhill 2007.

12. We use "assess" and "evaluate" interchangeably, though the former may involve more informal processes while the latter is usually more formal. "Measurement," however, refers to more precise ways of determining effectiveness or success and, in conventional research, normally involves quantifying results or outcomes.

13. Coffman's 2009 paper on current practices served as background for a conference of 120 advocates, evaluators and funders discussing advocacy evaluation advances.

14. See also Actionaid <actionaid.org>, which has long been at the forefront of this work.

15. Stachowiak (2009) has produced a summary of six social science theories that have relevance to advocacy and change efforts. All are directed at institutional or policy change as key to large social change. These are: punctuated equilibrium theory (significant changes occur when conditions are right); coalition theory (policy change happens through coordinated activity); agenda setting theory (change happens when advocates can connect components of the policy process); prospect theory (the key to changing views is the framing of options); power elites theory (change is made by working directly with power elites); and community organizing theory (change is made through grassroots collective action).

16. As Patton notes, there is "evidence that some problems and weaknesses can be easier to surface when evaluation takes an appreciative stance" (2003: 91). For further discussion on appreciative inquiry see, for example, Bushe 1998; Dick 2004; Dick 2006; Elliot 1999; Cooperrider and Whitney 2005; Ludema et al. 2001; Patton 2003; Robinson-Easley 1998; and Zandee and Cooperrider 2008. Action research and appreciative inquiry have become increasingly prominent in the evaluation field (Patton 2003; Patton 2010; Preskill and Catsambas 2006; Preskill and Coghlan 2003; Reason and Bradbury 2007).

17. The "dream" phase of this process addresses the criticism that AI ignores "the negative." In the "dream" phase, people are asked to envision a positive future, implicitly providing information about what they see as deficits in the current reality.

18. This included a notice in the bulletin of the Canadian Council on International Cooperation, a coalition of NGOs in Canada. CCIC had a monthly "flash bulletin" that included brief announcements, such as our invitation to activist organizations to participate.

19. Interviews were taped and transcribed, and then coded and managed with the assistance of a qualitative software package (ATLASti). At least two researchers coded each interview.

3

OXFAM CANADA

THE "FAIR TRADE IN COFFEE" CAMPAIGN

Bill Hynd and Carol Miller

> In our community there wasn't a lot of awareness about fair trade coffee when we first started campaigning about ten years ago. We would set up display boards, produce hand-out materials and do media work and interviews. Basically we talked to any group interested in hearing about fair trade coffee. We also encouraged our supporters to ask for fair trade coffee at local coffee shops and restaurants. Of course, we knew full well that none was available so we would simply leave behind a fact sheet on coffee along with a phone number where fair trade coffee could be ordered. And then we persuaded our local natural food store to bring in fair trade coffee. This made our campaigning efforts easier as we could direct people to the food store. Of course things have changed dramatically over the past ten years as today our town now has a fair trade coffee roaster. By no means can we take credit for the fact the Loblaws and Dominion stores now carry all these fair trade products. However I would like to think Oxfam played a fairly significant role in getting fair trade onto the public agenda. (Oxfam Campaigner)

About Oxfam Canada

Oxfam Canada[1] seeks to build lasting solutions to global poverty and injustice. It works with allies in Canada and around the world to change the policies and practices that perpetuate human suffering. In Africa, the Americas and Asia it works with over one hundred partner organizations to tackle the root causes of poverty, injustice and inequality, helping to create self-reliant and sustainable communities, with a specific focus on women rights and gender equality. In Canada, Oxfam is involved in development education, advocacy, public awareness and building a constituency of support for its goal to advance women's rights.

Oxfam Canada believes Canadians and other citizens of the world can end poverty and injustice by working together in solidarity to assert their basic human rights. It seeks to mobilize public support for changing the policies that perpetuate poverty. Oxfam Canada is also a founding member of Oxfam International, the federation of fourteen Oxfams worldwide. By working together, Oxfams believe they can significantly increase the impact and effectiveness of their individual programs.

Oxfam Canada has three distinct but inter-related change strategies, all of which came into play for the "Fair Trade in Coffee" campaign: these are campaigning for change, policy and advocacy and public engagement. With Oxfam International, Oxfam Canada engages in joint campaigns to raise awareness of issues relating to global poverty, and to influence the policy of governments and institutions such as the World Bank, the International Monetary Fund, the United Nations, the G8 and the World Trade Organization. It is worth noting, as well, that Oxfam's policy and advocacy work is closely linked to its development program and practice. Oxfam's advocacy and campaigns for just trade policies are rooted in the knowledge and experience gained through its development programming with poor communities and small-scale farmers, for example. Oxfam's position in the international community enables it to tap into institutional and governmental players that communities may need to realize change.

While Oxfam Canada comes from an activist tradition, it has always invested considerable energy in policy research, analysis and dialogue. On its own and as a participant in Canadian coalitions, Oxfam has played a leadership role in discussions on aid, trade, debt and development. It has also engaged with the Department of Foreign Affairs and International Trade and the Canadian International Development Agency in Ottawa, at the United Nations and in the field to influence Canada's foreign policy and aid program and to change the policies and practices of other governments.

Oxfam Canada devotes considerable energies to working within Canada, not just to mobilize resources but to actively engage Canadians in ideas, debate and action to address the inequalities that underlie poverty and injustice around the world and here in Canada. Staff working from regional offices support a network of thousands of volunteers who are actively engaged in campaigns, for example, by making presentations to schools and university students, circulating petitions, sending e-letters, organizing workshops, staging media events and meeting with Members of Parliament. Oxfam Canada clubs or groups have been active in anywhere from twenty to thirty university campuses or schools in recent years, and there are local committees in large and small communities across the country.

Fair Trade in Coffee

> The "Make Trade Fair" campaign was developed by Oxfam International. We promoted it full force across the country. (Oxfam campaigner)

The Oxfam International "Make Trade Fair" campaign focused on pressing governments and decision makers to adopt fairer trade rules that would make a real and positive difference in the fight against poverty. One of the more successful components of this overall campaign was specific work for "Fair Trade in Coffee." The overall campaign was carried out mainly between 2002 and 2006.[2] However, success certainly didn't happen all at once. Rather, there were specific moments and victories as well as more gradual but equally significant changes over the past decade in public awareness and attitudes about fair trade in coffee.

Ten Percent Coffee

Oxfam had become concerned about the impact of the sharp drop in the price of coffee beans — fifty percent between 1999 and 2002 — that had all but destroyed the livelihoods of some 25 million coffee producers. Under the existing system of coffee trade, very little of what consumers pay for coffee, often less than ten percent, reaches the farmer who grows the beans. Of the 25 million coffee producers worldwide, approximately 15 million are small farmers, mainly poor smallholders. Unable to export directly, they would sell their crops to mid-level traders, or as they are commonly called in Central America, "coyotes." These traders often used their monopoly position to pressure the farmer to sell low. These traders also provide loans to the farmers to assist with purchases. As lenders, these "coyotes" can and do demand extremely high interest payments. This type of exploitation resulted in a spiralling debt cycle leaving farmers and families further impoverished. The fall in the price of coffee — the "coffee crisis" — forced coffee farmers in developing countries to sell at a heavy loss, leaving them in a desperate position. Many small farmers were unable to cover their families' most basic needs, with families going hungry, children forced out of school and health status declining. In such dire circumstances many farmers had to sell their land and leave behind their homes and families in search of work elsewhere.[3]

The story of one Ethiopian coffee farmer interviewed by Oxfam in March 2002 paints a graphic picture of how the price collapse affected his family:

> Five to seven years ago, I was producing seven sacks of red cherry [unprocessed coffee] and this was enough to buy clothes, medicines, services and to solve so many problems. But now even if I sell four times as much, it is impossible to cover all my expenses. I had to sell my oxen to repay the loan I previously took out to buy fertilizers and improved seed for my corn, or face prison. Medical expenses are very high as this is a malaria-affected area. At least one member of my household has to

go to hospital each year for treatment. It costs $6 U.S. per treatment. We also need to buy teff [staple starch], salt, sugar, soap, kerosene for lighting. We have to pay for schooling. Earlier we could cover expenses, now we can't... three of the children can't go to school because I can't afford the uniform. We have stopped buying teff and edible oil. We are eating mainly corn. The children's skin is getting dry and they are showing signs of malnutrition. (Oxfam America 2002: 10)

At the same time as coffee producers were suffering, coffee sales and profits were rising. Oxfam's campaign helped to show there is an alternative and that the coffee market could work for the poor as well as the rich. Fairly traded coffee bought directly from farming cooperatives, thereby eliminating the role of the midlevel trader, would allow farmers to earn a reasonable living.

What Did Oxfam Do?

Oxfam focused on challenging the stranglehold the global coffee giants had on smaller coffee farmers and engaged in a variety of actions globally and across Canada. The work in the community ranged from setting up displays at university campuses and in church basements to media interviews. Many of the actions were taken up by individual Oxfam members and volunteers. Two inter-related strategies were used: campaigning for global policy change in how the coffee industry functioned and public engagement to change consumer awareness and practice at the local level.

Challenging the Global Coffee Giants

As part of the "Make Trade Fair" campaign, beginning in 2002, Oxfam challenged the four major coffee companies Kraft, Nestle, Proctor & Gamble and Sara Lee — who were making huge profits, each with over $1 billion a year in sales — to pay their respective coffee producers a fair and living wage. The big four roasters, along with Starbucks, had shown interest in responsible sourcing and some were already sourcing small amounts of coffee on fair trade terms. One of Oxfam's demands was that these companies purchase at least two percent of their coffee through certified fair trade sources. With no global coffee companies headquartered in Canada, Oxfam Canada initially targeted Kraft Canada with a postcard campaign, demanding that it share its profits with small coffee producers. As a result of its own research into the situation in Canada, Oxfam determined it should focus on engaging the Coffee Association of Canada (CAC — the national trade association representing the coffee industry in Canada) to push them to support socially responsible practices.

While the CAC was cautious of our emphasis on changing practices of the coffee industry, it was willing to join us to lobby the Canadian government to recommit to the International Coffee Organization (ICO). The ICO is the main intergovernmental organization for coffee, bringing together producing and consuming countries to tackle the challenges facing the world coffee sector through international cooperation (see ico.org/mission.asp). Canada had withdrawn from the ICO in 1990, rejecting its support for a coffee quota system whereby coffee supplies in excess of consumer requirements were withheld from the market. The ICO operated the quota system on and off from 1962 to 1989 when the system was suspended because of failure to agree on quota distribution. At that time, Canada was a major promoter of "free trade" agreements. The CAC was well aware of the crisis facing small coffee producers and agreed with Oxfam that the coffee crisis would best be resolved at the level of the ICO. Oxfam worked with the CAC to push Canada, via the Minister of Agriculture, to reconsider its position on the ICO. As a result, the two seemingly unlikely allies co-edited a piece in the *Globe and Mail* in June 2003 that called on Canada to address the disparities among coffee growing nations and global companies, concluding that: "Canada can help in the search for solutions. Joining the ICO is a first step" (Stuart and McAlpine 2003: A19).[4] While such efforts succeeded in encouraging Canada's Minister of Agriculture to reconsider Canada's position on the ICO, in the end Canada decided not to rejoin.[5] Nonetheless, this campaigning effort did promote change, but at a very different level: on university campuses where the engagement of students in Oxfam's demand for national policy change resulted in changes in consumer attitudes and behaviour at the local level.

Also in connection with the "Make Trade Fair" campaign, in 2006 Oxfam International launched a campaign to persuade Starbucks to sign a royalty-free licensing agreement that would recognize Ethiopia's right to control how its own coffee names are used, including fine coffees that had been sold under Starbucks' premium lines. In 2005 the Ethiopian government filed applications to trademark its most famous coffees, *Sidamo*, *Harar* and *Yirgacheffe*. Securing rights to these coffees would enable Ethiopia to capture more value from the trade by controlling their use in the market and thereby enable farmers to receive a greater share of the retail price (Oxfam Canada 2006a). Ethiopia had successfully registered trademarks with governments in Canada, the European Union and Japan. Parallel to registering the brands with other countries, the Ethiopian government was seeking agreements with coffee roasters acknowledging Ethiopians' right to control these brands. Ownership over the names would result in greater control over how the beans are marketed and would ultimately result in a greater share of the profits going to the fifteen million poor people in Ethiopia who are dependent on that crop.

> [Starbucks was] essentially blocking the Ethiopian government from trademarking their own regional coffee brands. But it's actually coffee grown in a particular Ethiopian region. Starbucks was fighting the government's ability to essentially trademark their own regional province names. (Oxfam campaigner)

Aware of Starbucks' status as a global brand interested in maintaining its reputation as a socially responsible company, Oxfam had begun negotiating with Starbucks in 2005 when it first learned about Ethiopia's efforts to trademark its fine coffees. After dozens of conversations between Oxfam America's Boston headquarters, the Seattle home of Starbucks and Ethiopia's Intellectual Property Office in Addis Ababa, it became clear that high-level talks would not be enough to resolve the trademark issue.

It Was Time to Enlist the Public

At a grassroots level, Oxfam supporters worked with a coalition of allies including members of the Ethiopian diaspora, students, faith-based groups and even some Starbucks employees. By the campaign's end, more than 100,000 people worldwide had gotten involved (Oxfam America 2007).

In Canada, the campaign provided a platform to raise public awareness about fair trade issues. On December 15, 2006 activists across Canada — in unison with activists around the world — held demonstrations outside Starbucks to protest the company's refusal to recognize the rights of Ethiopian coffee farmers to the names of their own coffees. The actions formed part of a global day of solidarity with Ethiopian farmers who produce world-class coffee, but who continue to live in poverty. As one Oxfam Canada (2006b) press release put it, "Starbucks loudly proclaims its commitment to the welfare of the farmers who provide it with world-class coffee... we'll know that sentiment is genuine when they acknowledge Ethiopia's ownership of its coffee names." Bowing in part to worldwide pressure, by June 2007 Starbucks and the Government of Ethiopia eventually reached an agreement which recognized Ethiopians' right to control the use of their speciality coffee brands. It was described by Oxfam Canada (2007) as a "victory for all sides, because this agreement has the potential to give farmers a fairer share of the profits... which should help improve the lives of millions of poor farmers, allowing them to send their children to school and access healthcare."

Engaging Canadians

Oxfam's work to bring about policy change nationally and internationally has gone hand in hand with work to raise public awareness about fair trade. During the past decade or so Oxfam Canada has worked hard to educate Canadians about how important fair trade is for poor farming communities overseas. Our strategy has been to engage local people in local actions. This enabled people to recognize that they have a responsibility as well as opportunities to affect change here in Canada.

> I think that in all the work we do, raising public awareness... is the most fundamental thing. If people don't know, they're not going to work for change... that's a central core to our work — educating people for action. [We help to show them] this is the problem, this is the solution and this is how you can be part of the solution. (Oxfam campaigner)

Some regional offices trained their volunteers to effectively become fair trade ambassadors: equipped with knowledge and information about the "Make Trade Fair" and "Fair Trade in Coffee" campaigns, they promoted the cause in their communities and on their campuses. As more and more people in the community became aware of the issues, Oxfam became, in some regions, a go-to point for unions and local businesses. In Vancouver, for example, Oxfam took the lead in establishing a Fair Trade Coffee Network. Through the network, Oxfam continued to promote fair trade coffee, going to coffee shops and supermarkets and trying to encourage them to supply fair trade products.

> With the "Fair Trade in Coffee" campaign] one of the things that makes it very effective is that it's an issue that people see really affects their own lives… the fact is they drink coffee. So it's not something that is totally obscure or seems totally irrelevant to their own lives. And so they relate to it on a very personal level. (Oxfam campaigner)

One of the very tangible outcomes of engaging Canadians on global on trade issues has been awareness raising about practical actions that can be taken at the local level. For example, university clubs have taken the lead in pushing to have fair trade coffee readily available on their campuses. At Memorial University in Newfoundland, for example, Oxfam staff and campus members persuaded the main coffee vendor on campus to include a fair trade coffee.

> We didn't achieve the policy change we were asking for. But we succeeded in huge awareness raising and we created a huge movement on campuses and in our communities to promote fair trade coffee and raise awareness about the plight [of farmers due to the drop in] commodity prices. (Oxfam campaigner)

Oxfam's primary ally in advancing fair trade amongst Canadians was TransFair Canada. TransFair Canada (refer online to transfair.ca) is Canada's only non-profit certification and public education organization promoting Fair Trade Certified to improve the livelihood of developing world farmers and workers. They assisted in working with Oxfam campus clubs across the country to promote fair trade on their respective campuses. Today, it is difficult to find a coffee shop on a university campus in Canada that does not sell fair trade coffee. Some universities even took the step of adopting fair trade policies stipulating that any company selling coffee on campus had to make fair trade coffee available.

What Works in Campaigns, Advocacy and Public Engagement?

What factors have contributed to success in advocacy and public engagement work undertaken by Oxfam Canada? The graphic below outlines the broad level indicators of success or effectiveness in advocacy and influencing work.

Clearly, several of the indicators relate to specific change strategies, each often with different targets (for example, government, big business, public or other NGOs). Nonetheless, the graphic suggests a relationship between success in one area and success in another in an overall vision of success in social justice change work. In other words, the different areas can be seen as mutually reinforcing parts of a whole. The stories about the "Fair Trade in Coffee" campaign, for example, illustrate the relationship between short sharp campaigns with clearly defined high-level targets and long-term, low-level campaigning and public engagement activities aimed at raising public awareness and attitudes.

"Good reputation and credibility" (Oxfam campaigner) — in other words, having Oxfam Canada "recognised as a credible voice for change" (Oxfam campaigner) — is one key indicator of success. This involves, for example, invitations to participate or to input expertise into key decision-making processes and events. Without credibility to speak on the issues being addressed and a good reputation amongst key stakeholders it is very difficult to have one's voice heard and to make an impact.

"Good relationships" are also important to successful outcomes of advocacy and influencing work in their own right, alongside the more standard indicators of success, such as increased public awareness and policy impact. These include relationships among internal staff members, in the case of Oxfam Canada, particularly between campaigners and development program staff working with partners in the field, as well as with external actors and stakeholders. Key characteristics of such relationships include mutual respect,

Figure 3.1

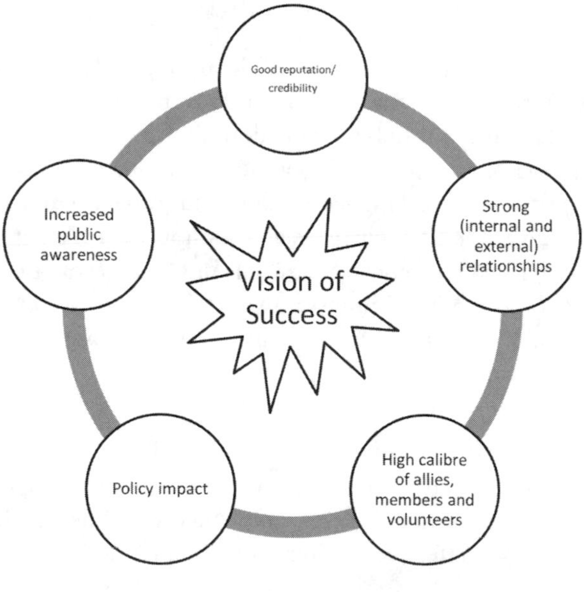

shared values and purpose and clarity on roles and responsibilities. Good relationships are not only considered as a factor contributing to effectiveness in advocacy and influencing, but at the individual level contribute to a sense of being part of something and a sense of cohesiveness.

Another critical aspect is the need to unpack the notion of policy impact in order to better measure success in this area: for example, differentiating between success in terms of tangible policy changes (for example, changing trade rules around coffee) and success in relation to policy implementation (such as how far the changes in the rules of trade are implemented on the ground). The latter requires ongoing civil society monitoring, which, in the Canadian context, can be achieved with the support of a "high calibre cohort." This can refer to knowledgeable and engaged members and volunteers or to credible, respected allies, for example the Canadian Coffee Association with whom Oxfam partnered to lobby the government around re-joining the ICO.

"Increased public awareness" encompasses both changes in knowledge levels as well as changes in practice (that is, what is done with that knowledge). It is far easier to monitor and evaluate policy change than changes in attitudes and behaviours, which may happen over many years, if not generations. In the case of the "Fair Trade in Coffee" campaign, for example, there is significant anecdotal information to suggest that both attitudes and practice changed in the space of a decade. Attracting and retaining high calibre volunteers as an indicator of success is also essential, as this enhances our capacity as well as creates a foundation for long-term engagement needed to bring about social justice goals.

For Oxfam Canada, success or effectiveness of advocacy and influencing work would ultimately be measured in relation to how far a contribution has been made to achieving the goal of ending poverty and injustice, particularly gender inequality.

Oxfam Canada Change Strategies: Lessons Learned

Figure 3.2 offers one way of conceptualizing the key factors that can contribute to success in advocacy, campaigns and public engagement work. Key to this approach is the recognition that effectiveness in social justice advocacy work requires us to look beyond the effectiveness of our work itself to consider the impact of a wider range of factors.

"Effective advocacy and campaigns" is one element — albeit a crucial one — in effective social justice influencing work. What are some key factors that contribute to effective advocacy and campaigns? It must be based on credible research and policy analysis. In the "Fair Trade in Coffee" campaign, for example, research on the impact of the terms of trade on coffee farmers was essential to making the case for policy change. Policy research, however,

Figure 3.2

needs to be translated into policy papers and policy positions, which, in the case of the "Fair Trade in Coffee" campaign, was an important role played by Oxfam International, with its ability to mobilize researchers and policy development teams across the affiliates to identify key targets and policy recommendations. Related to this, Oxfam recognized the importance of setting targets that are achievable and time-bound. In a long-term struggle such as that for global fair trade, breaking down actions and targets into short-term, achievable goals is absolutely crucial to sustain energy and commitment; for example, through the focused campaign to change the practices of Starbucks.

Another factor that contributes to successful advocacy is Oxfam's strategy of engagement at different levels and in different arenas — global, national and local. In the "Make Trade Fair" campaign, for example, Oxfam worked to promote policy change at the World Trade Organization, with national governments, at coffee corporation shareholder meetings, through the media, in the courts and in the streets. This is an important benefit of working within the Oxfam International confederation; individually, it would be difficult for Oxfams to sustain effective engagement across these multiple levels.

Good knowledge about the targets of a campaign is also important. Oxfam was aware, for example, that the big coffee roasters, Starbucks in particular, had corporate responsibility charters for which they could be called to account. Oxfam Canada was able to articulate a Canadian angle on a global issue — another strategy it regularly adopts to be effective in advocacy and campaigning work. In the case of the "Fair Trade in Coffee" campaign, Oxfam lobbied the Canadian government to re-join the ICO and also raised awareness amongst consumers in Canada that how and where they choose to buy their coffee can affect a global brand. A good campaign provides people with actions that they can take to advance the cause. The more localized the action, the easier it is to engage people directly. Too many global campaigns rely on petition signatures which do not sufficiently engage activists, who are often willing to do much more to support a cause they believe in.

Finally, effective advocacy and campaigning work requires us to be attentive to when the timing is right and to be ready to act when opportunities arise. For instance, in the "Fair Trade in Coffee" campaign, Oxfam attempted to react quickly to any media publicity on coffee or coffee companies by writing letters to the editor to highlight the fair trade cause. Oxfam mobilized around shareholders meetings, too, to provide concise information sheets about its requests.

Another factor of success relates to "effective public engagement work." Oxfam Canada's public engagement strategy seeks to build a base of activists through public education and awareness initiatives. Public education fosters a clear understanding of issues and the ability to act on these issues. What factors contribute to effective public engagement? Oxfam Canada attempts to link local actions with global issues, making it clear that individual Canadians can and do have an impact on what happens globally. The Starbucks campaign, particularly the day of solidarity with Ethiopian farmers in December 2006, is a good example of this. We have also learned that it is important to design initiatives that are creative, practical, well-organized and fun. For example, the December 16, 2006 day of solidarity engaged volunteers standing outside busy Starbucks shops in four cities across the country in rousing verses of a song sung to the tune of Winter Wonderland:

> Starbucks are you listening,
> Across the world folks are bristling
> It's time that you cared
> It's time that you shared
> Your profits with the folks in poorer lands
> Starbucks — have you no shame
> Sidamo's not your name
> The coffee on display
> Costs more than you pay
> To the farmers in this far-off land

The "Fair Trade in Coffee" campaign illustrates Oxfam Canada's ability to mobilize its diverse base of volunteers and members across the country. By tapping into the energy, creativity and diversity of its supporters, Oxfam Canada has been able to reach out beyond a committed core to engage a wide spectrum of Canadians from different regions, ages and ethnic, racial and social backgrounds. Oxfam Canada is aware that much of the public engagement work in which it is involved depends on volunteers and that their contribution must be valued and acknowledged.

Public engagement work is often carried out in parallel with and seen as mutually reinforcing advocacy and campaigns. In other words, Oxfam Canada tries to take a joined-up approach across a range of actions. This was certainly the case in the "Fair Trade in Coffee" campaign, for example, where policy advocacy targeting government and big business not only engaged the public as a means of putting pressure on key actors, but raised public awareness aware about fair trade coffee and contributed to changed consumer behaviour.

In its advocacy and campaigning, Oxfam Canada works in partnerships and alliances with other like-minded nongovernmental organizations (NGOs) within Canada, in other countries or globally, as well as with local community-based organizations. In the "Fair Trade in Coffee" campaign, for example, not only did Oxfam work with multinationals, roasters, retailers, like-minded NGOs, consumers and policy makers to influence the terms of trade, markets, regulations and consumer attitudes, but it also provided support to coffee producers, individually and collectively, to strengthen their capacity to organize, produce, market, negotiate and defend their rights. Such partnerships can be described as "adding value by amplifying voice," "increasing connections with communities" and "building on the strengths of each partner" (Oxfam campaigners). As with its overseas program, Oxfam Canada increases the impact of campaign and advocacy work by collaborating closely with Oxfam International. In the case of the "Make Trade Fair" campaign, for example, more than eighteen million people around the world, most of them from the South, signed a petition demanding that the World Trade Organization negotiate terms of trade that promote development. Oxfam Canada's ability to bring a Canadian perspective to the framing of these global campaigns and to adapt the analysis and materials of a global campaign to the Canadian reality represents a significant contribution and benefit, as was evident in the work around "Fair Trade in Coffee." But even more exciting, Oxfam Canada's ability to link concerned Canadians with like-minded citizens of other countries North and South provided a tremendous opportunity to build solidarity and a deeper understanding of common cause.

The factors that facilitate meaningful, reciprocal partnerships Oxfam has identified include: recognition that partners are equal actors in strategizing and decision making; engaging a diverse mix of people, expertise and experiences; effective communications; and flexibility. In the "Fair Trade in Coffee" campaign, for example, there was considerable flexibility required in working with partners as diverse as the Coffee Association, which represents the overall coffee industry, and TransFair Canada, which represents fair trade coffee producers and sellers, mostly small players in the coffee industry. Each organization was involved in different sets of actions that were in line with their respective missions and values, but were able to come together for joint efforts, for example, to lobby the Minister of Agriculture for Canada to re-join the ICO, and to raise awareness of Canada's position in relation to global coffee trade rules.

One of the challenges for Oxfam Canada, like many other organizations carrying out advocacy and campaigning work, is that there are significant concerns and issues around which it could engage. However, it recognizes that competing demands means it is important to recognize limitations as well as strengths and make the most of resources. More and more, it does this by focusing our energies on issues where Oxfam can provide added value and a high chance of success. It aims to make more effective use of people's time and skills, inspire greater motivation and creativity and achieve increased impact. In the "Make Trade Fair" campaign, one example of Oxfam focusing its energies was at the 2002 G8 Summit held in Kananaskis, Alberta.

> We organized for volunteers to come from all over Canada, for all of the [Oxfam] Canadian Program Team to come and we also hosted an Oxfam International delegation of about twenty people. And so we were all focused on one event with many, many different layers. So there were the advocacy people... the media centers and... lobbying of officials. There were people who were organizing high profile media stunts [often involving] the volunteers. When they weren't, they were involved in trade workshops that we were giving and going over our plans for upcoming Make Trade Fair campaigns. There was just a real sense of cohesiveness that we were all working toward the same purpose. And we could see every night on the news if we were successful, if we got media attention and our particular voice was heard. And it quite often was. (Oxfam campaigner)

Oxfam has recognized, as well, the need for greater overall focus as an organization. In 2005, strategic review and planning processes within Oxfam and with external allies resulted in a major decision within Oxfam Canada: "We believe the most effective way to strengthen our program — and advance our mission — is to focus our resources and expertise in support of women's rights and gender equality."[6] The current Oxfam Canada Strategic Plan (2007-2012), "Walking the Talk on Women's Rights," articulates the organization's new focus, building on ground work that had been carried out in previous decades. This has helped to give Oxfam Canada strategic direction in its advocacy, campaigning and public engagement work as it seeks to increase effectiveness and impact.

The role that "internal systems and practices" play in supporting effective social justice influencing and advocacy work should not be underestimated. Everything from the governance structure to internal communications to monitoring, evaluation and learning systems impact on effectiveness in social justice advocacy work. For an organization such as Oxfam Canada, where campaigns, advocacy and public engagement work in Canada must link closely with the work it does with Southern partners, it is important to have good systems and structures that facilitate cross-organizational working and exchange of knowledge and perspectives across different teams. Related to this is the need for internal communications that articulate clearly the organizational goals and priorities.

Taking time to stop and reflect on whether or not these broader systems and practices are facilitating effective advocacy and campaigning work is not easy, especially in a large organization with staff and volunteers scattered across the country. Too often systematic monitoring, evaluation and learning gets ignored in the immediacy of advocacy and campaigning work — though it is regularly carried out on an ad hoc basis by individual staff. For this reason, Oxfam Canada has in recent years prioritized and increased resources and strategies for monitoring, evaluating and learning to facilitate program development and the sharing of success stories, including the hiring of specialist staff.

Half-Empty or Half-Full: Oxfam Canada's Campaigning [Coffee] Cup

In 2006, one Oxfam Canada campaigner wrote a reflective piece for his colleagues, "Oxfam Canada's Campaigning Cup: Is it Half-Empty or Half-Full?" (Oxfam Canada 2006c). In it, he evaluated several Oxfam campaigns from "Education Now," which focused on the right to education for all, to "No Sweat," which promoted labour rights as human rights, to the "Make Trade Fair" campaign. The article provides a glimpse of the kinds of changes or impacts that are equated with success of social advocacy and influencing work, including: new awareness by policy makers of human rights issues; changed policy (globally through the UN and nationally in the Canadian context); credibility for Oxfam Canada as an actor at key policy-making tables; raised awareness amongst Canadians; and engagement by the public as active citizens in promoting change. The piece asked whether or not, taken together, these successes resulted in "real" change in the achievement of human rights or the eradication of poverty.

Posed perhaps as a rhetorical question, the piece nonetheless suggests that all these successes do contribute to real change and, as such, it is important to recognize and celebrate them while at the same time acknowledging that real change may appear elusive in the short term. This is a crucial point to keep in focus, particularly in the current international development funding context, in which public (state) resources for advocacy work are increasingly difficult to secure. We hope that the story of the campaign for "Fair Trade in Coffee" suggests that Oxfam's metaphorical "campaigning cup" is at least half-full, if not overflowing.[7]

Notes

1. More information about Oxfam Canada can be found online at <oxfam.ca>.
2. For further information on the ongoing efforts of Oxfam to "Make Trade Fair" through campaigning on global trade rules and targeting the G8 and key international institutions, see <oxfam.ca/what-we-do/campaigns/make-trade-fair>. For specific work carried out in relation to "Fair Trade in Coffee" see <oxfam.ca/what-we-do/campaigns/fair-trade-in-coffee>.
3. For a full analysis of the impact of the "coffee crisis" during this period see: Oxfam America, 2002, "Mugged: Poverty in Your Coffee Cup," at <oxfamamerica.org/publications/mugged-poverty-in-your-coffee-cup>.
4. The ICO and the coffee industry are currently considering a new global coffee purchasing code. Oxfam International is actively monitoring the details of the new code.
5. A similar campaign in the U.S. was more successful. In 2004, the U.S. decided to rejoin the ICO, eleven years after it left in 1993 (Oxfam America 2004).
6. For more information on our decision to focus on gender equality and women's rights, see our Strategic Plan at <oxfam.ca/what-we-do>.
7. We would like to thank Robert Fox, Executive Director of Oxfam Canada, Elizabeth Whitmore, Maureen G. Wilson and Avery Calhoun, for their helpful comments on earlier drafts. The responsibility for the opinions expressed in this chapter rests solely with the authors and does not represent Oxfam Canada policy.

4

THE DISABILITY ACTION HALL

TELL STORIES, TAKE ACTION, CHANGE LIVES

Ryan Geake, Colleen Huston and members of the Action Hall

Brodie, a new member of the Disability Action Hall, was asked at the meeting to make a sign for the upcoming Disability Pride Parade. Brodie wrote his idea down on his tablet: "I am tired of people calling me disabled." Brodie's sign sparked an enthusiastic discussion among members about how, as disabled persons, we struggle to be proud of our disability. A member suggested to Brodie, "Disability is not a dirty word." Brodie screams in delight and starts making the new sign. Having a sign about pride would not have happened ten years ago.

This photo is at our "Speak Out," our eleventh annual pride celebration at the Olympic Plaza in Calgary. Inset is Brodie facing the crowd wearing a sign saying, "Disability is Not a Dirty Word." Many people from the disability community, partners, politicians and friends attended the event to celebrate disability pride and culture. A pride parade followed down the city's outdoor mall. Vern Reynolds-Braun photo

Celebrating Disability Pride at the local Plaza movie theatre for our 10th annual Speak Out Event.
Ryan Geake photo

The Story of the Action Hall

> It is great to have a disability community. People in that community know exactly what I am talking about when I say that I was called a "retard" at school. They know because they were called that too. People without disabilities may not understand that because they have never experienced that label. (Jennifer Stewart, Action Hall member)

The story of the Action Hall is a story of accomplishment for the developmental disability community in Calgary. It is a group that has had some success at exploring the ideas of disability culture, pride and identity, creating a safe place for disabled people to be who they are, and taking action on systemic issues impacting disabled Albertans.

Prior to the existence of the Action Hall, disabled people in the city of Calgary didn't see themselves as part of a separate community with its own identity, goals, experiences and dreams. Disabled people existed together in social ways such as in the Special Olympics, in services to assist with daily living or, on rare occasions, as individuals asked to consult on the disability experience. There was a limited political understanding that disabled people were a minority group and thus needed to act accordingly.

The Right to Gather

> Many of the experiences of people with disabilities in Canada were based on exclusion and difference. They were treated as less than other citizens. (Stienstra and Wight-Felskey 2003: 5)

A number of philosophical perspectives on disability have influenced, over time, how disabled people have been treated. These have included a medical model focused only on the imperfection of the body, a charity model that sees disability as a reason for pity and the currently prevailing model of integrating disabled people into the community. The latter communicates to disabled people, workers in the field and the wider community that success for disabled people means a seamless fit into the non-disabled community. From this perspective, disability workers are actually barriers to this inclusion, and ultimately the community should assume the support of disabled people. Definitions of success in this model involve disabled people attaining the status symbols of their non-disabled community members such as a job, material goods, as much independence as possible and few or no services — in essence to be as non-disabled as possible. Disability is a source of shame and something to be overcome or at least hidden. Inherent in the community inclusion model is the critique of any gathering of disabled people, as this is believed to create further marginalization.

In the Action Hall's desire to shift toward a "disability pride" orientation, the first concern encountered was that of our right to assemble. Disabled people, workers and organizations needed to see themselves and their work differently. A re-conceptualization of who and what we were was essential if there was to be an impact on the lives of disabled people in our city. Removing the "inclusion" lens and replacing it with a "minority group" lens began slowly through the teachings of other minority groups. We watched films on the civil rights movement and learned about people like Rosa Parks. We educated ourselves about disability groups who were challenging stereotypes and government policy and holding protests. Groups such as American Disabled for Attendant Programs Today and disabled artists like Cheryl Marie Wade became our mentors and heroes.

Alongside of developing a culture of action, we were having regular conversations about our feelings as disabled people. Ideas such as "disability is natural" or "the disability experience has things to teach the world" became topics to explore and think about. Labelling ourselves with the disability tag was also part of the discussion and very difficult for many members of the Action Hall. The strong sense of shame that has been synonymous with disability had to be discussed and challenged, and new ways of identifying ourselves had to be tried on. People actually practiced telling each other that they had a disability. We were on the journey to pride!

Kelly and His Budget

Many stories of this consciousness raising have become part of the folklore of the Action Hall. One of the memorable stories told is called "Kelly and His Budget." Kelly was puzzled about why he could not live on $20 per week for spending money. He believed he had a budgeting problem and needed some counselling for this. Other members started talking about themselves as bad budgeters as well. When an ally suggested that no one in Calgary could live on $20 a week, members, over a number of meetings, turned their individual budgeting problem into a story of common poverty. Allies helped to re-frame the concern from an individual problem to the structural issue that social assistance incomes were not enough to live on. We discussed why disabled people should be forced to live in poverty and if they deserved it. These conversations moved from taking a budgeting class and getting counselling, to becoming angry with our poverty and questioning if we could do something about it. Similar discussions took place on accessible affordable housing, the inadequate transportation system, the lack of opportunities for love and friendship and the erosion of social services. Through the inspiration of other groups standing up for themselves, we began to believe we could too.

Speak Out

The process of liberation is one from victim to survivor to warrior. —source unknown

---

Back in 1998 when the above conversation was occurring we agreed that we needed to learn through action also. We decided to put on a rally. We named it "Speak Out." At the same time that our rally was being planned, the Alberta Government was taking ten million dollars out of services to people with disabilities. Our rally turned into the first of many community actions on this issue, including a petition, a letter writing campaign, more protests in Calgary and at the legislature in Edmonton and eventually a town hall meeting with the Minister in charge of the sector.

Action Hall members got excited about taking action on such issues and felt empowered by all of the learning that was taking place. Most importantly, we tasted success. Through the work of the Action Hall, and with the support of a number of agencies, the government put the ten million dollars back into the system. People experienced the power of meeting together, eating together, learning together and taking action together — from being alone to celebrating as a collective.

Why We Feel Successful as a Group

> If we've learned anything from other oppressed minorities, it's that you gain nothing from efforts to assimilate into the culture that devalues you. We will never be equal if we accept token acceptance as slightly damaged able bodies. Holistically and psychologically our power will come from celebrating who we are as a distinct people. I'm not content being a pale version of the majority culture. I want to be a strong version of something else — different but equally valid. (Gill 1994: 49)

One of the successes of the Action Hall is that we embrace the theory of how social movements create change. We understand that social movements happen when people stand up and take action over issues that were once deeply personalized as their fault. People find common characteristics of oppression in their stories and they begin to understand that the problems they experienced are not their fault. The sources of the issues are recognized as being in the societal structures that do not allow people equal access to many of the opportunities that other people may have. To begin to move from being passive persons who accept their fate to activists who want to create justice, we believe people have to go through the process of collective self identity, collective action on the issues that they want to work on and the development of an alternative sense of pride and culture. All of our work is based on the simplified understanding of how social movements have created amazing changes around the world.

Weekly Meetings for Fun, Food, and Work

When we reflected on the features of the success, we agreed that one of the features of the Action Hall that was critical for success was to have weekly meetings. We often joke that we meet weekly much like a church. People travel up to four hours each week despite the weather being freezing cold or blistering heat. Some come early to avoid rush hour. We have a meal together to start every meeting. Like all good meals, our meetings are full of jokes, teasing and informality following a natural rhythm of discussion. We like to work on a full stomach — after the meal, once we are full and satisfied, the work begins. Weekly meetings allow us to stay actively engaged and to respond quickly to the ever-changing political environment. Holding weekly gatherings allows us to watch the events, re-fashion messages and create new strategies on the issues we are engaged in.

The Power of Stories

The motto of the Action Hall is "Tell Stories, Take Action, Change Lives." The strength of the disability voice brought to lobbying efforts is the daily reality of living with a disability. An example of the disability voice successfully being heard took place at a standing policy committee meeting with senior MLAs where people with disabilities and allies presented on why an increase to social assistance commonly known as Assured Income for the Severely Handicapped (AISH) was needed. After many allies presented facts and figures, the story that changed the mood in the room was from a single mother with a disability, who was poorly dressed and had not been able to shower in days. She spoke through tears of not being able to buy her son a Christmas present. There was not a dry eye in the room. The minister responsible for AISH apologized profusely and said he would personally commit to do something about AISH. As a result, a province-wide review of the program was initiated by the Alberta Government.

Much of our success at the Disability Action Hall has been meeting like a family. Having fun and celebrating one another on a weekly basis is key to our success. Our group has been nurtured by food, as many Hall members who live in poverty also travel over three and a half to four hours to the weekly meeting. Food has been helpful to keep the group focus on social justice and to help stay in touch with one another.

Another successful feature is purposeful coalition building and the ability to quickly turn a personal story into collective action. For example, eight years ago one Action Hall member brought to a meeting a newspaper article about bus passes increasing by five dollars, explaining that she could not afford another increase. Many people were outraged and discussed what actions needed to be taken. We decided to go to Calgary Transit to learn whose door we should knock on. A few weeks later we spoke to the municipal committee responsible about the fare increase. City Council was so impressed with the stories from Action Hall members that they asked City staff to work with the Action Hall on a committee that would include municipal and provincial layers of government. We invited other poverty groups to those meetings, where we learned many people living in poverty were having a hard time affording the bus passes. Transportation policy advisors of the City informed us that we would have quicker success lobbying just for a disability bus pass, but collectively we decided to work together to lobby for a pass for all Calgarians living on low incomes. Although our fight may have taken longer, eight years later Calgary is the first city in Canada to have a transit pass for all low-income citizens. Thousands of people can now get around our city and it all began by the simple telling of a story, an action of one person bringing a newspaper article to a meeting.

Collective Engagement in Public Consultation and Policy Development

We believe that one of the successful features of the group is how we engage in public consultation and policy development as a collective. In the early days, as the Action Hall developed a reputation for expertise on disability issues, many members were asked to join different boards and committees related to our issues. We have to come to realize being a lone participant on these committees can lead to being co-opted, isolated and ineffective. Instead we have adopted the strategy of either ensuring an ally is present to help translate with the self-advocate during the meeting or having the consultation come to us as a collective. If allies and disabled people sit on particular committees, the Action Hall is able to help direct the efforts. It does not matter who is sitting at the table as the voice of the Action Hall is a collective voice of many.

Sustaining Ourselves

People often ask how we keep going. As one member says, "We have years of practice. We support each other and we are growing. We are like family." Maintaining the health and focus of the group means constant effort. Planning together, eating together and playing together are healthy ways to relieve tension and to keep ourselves motivated. The meetings are loosely structured, with food, jokes, announcements and the freedom to explore topics and feelings and go off on many tangents. People learn at different paces and there is a constant effort to make sure we understand the issues and keep a pace that is comfortable for everyone in the room. Sustainable engagement of the group and long-term relationships among the members are one of the unique successes of the Action Hall. A long time activist commented on how it is rare to see a group stay together for more than five years. Part of the reason for the group's ability to stay around is the variety of resources from a variety of places contributing to building success for the group.

Building a Disability Pride Movement

Some of the favourite stories of success told by Action Hall members have been about the Disability Pride Parades and the low-income transit pass. Both key initiatives have common characteristics such as engaging the community, opportunities to practice being proud, being experts about disability and helping the community.

By about 2003, following from these positive results for the Action Hall, our thirst to create new ways to influence the community was growing. We were influencing social policy and impacting the community by taking on new arts projects around social messaging and arts development. We also started to see some of the benefits of coalition work on low-income and public transportation. Some of the results of the efforts of members were reinforced by politicians mentioning the Action Hall in provincial reports, public consultations and culture jamming efforts such as our "poverty sucks" button, seeing our work on television during newscasts, having family members attend artists' performances and the rebuilding of personal relationships for members as their family members saw them in a place of power and pride. Action Hall members were asked to speak at conferences and in classrooms.

In 2003 the disability pride movement in the U.K. was given a surge of money for the International Year of Disabled Persons. This allowed us to tap into a network of strong disabled artists who were grounded in the social movement model, members of which were able to come to Calgary to mentor our members on being proud to be disabled. These workshops led to many conversations and public messages about being "loud and proud, louder and prouder." These disabled artists were strong and challenged the group to look at power, pride from within and building a civically engaged group to explore the use of the arts and other methods to define what disability culture is. The artists encouraged us to explore what we can do to build a community of strength and also challenge mainstream culture to redefine diversity. We were ready to look at disability pride.

> The "respect for who we are" has to start with us. We need to work on our own heads about who we are, our value and the value of our culture. When we develop a stronger identity as a community, we can really serve notice on society, or integrate into it, from a position of strength — on no one's terms but ours. (Gill 1994: 49)

After many years of building a safe place, we came to a point where the Action Hall was ready to deepen the conversations about self identity. We asked people, "Are you proud to be disabled?" As the question was answered around the table, one of the members said:

> I know my disability makes me who I am today, but if I could take a magic pill and my disability would go away instantly I would. I have lost friends, fought with family members, and cannot keep a job, I have been teased, bullied and was not able to graduate in school. I am tired of being different.

Other Action Hall members said:

> the [Action] Hall meetings are the only place during the week where I am proud to be who I am and where people understand what I am going through... I enjoy our pride parade, but I need to celebrate my disability every day. Why is it that we only celebrate pride once a year?

These inquiries opened up a fresh new set of questions, helped foster cross-disability public events like "Freak Out" (an annual disability cultural celebration in Calgary) and nurtured our daily struggle around how we can re-think powerlessness into power. In the words of one Action Hall member, Jennifer Stewart,

> I feel so proud of myself when I am on stage as a performer as an actor. I feel like I am on top of the world. But in everyday life I feel just... Disabled Jen. Then I went to a workshop and my mentor said this to me... she said, "It is up to you. You can turn that around. You can be Proud Disabled Jen in the everyday world."

The encounters that many Action Hall members have regularly reveal this belief that disability is somehow shameful. When people encounter the alternate belief, that disability can be a place of pride, they react with disbelief and challenge that notion quite directly. And so, when the "My Voice My Turn" project (a public marketing campaign about disability issues) was publicizing the slogan, "Proud to be Disabled," a woman said to Shelly, an Action Hall member who was staffing the display booth, "No one is proud to be disabled." Luckily, Thomas, an Action Hall member who had put forth that slogan, happened to walk up to the booth at the same time and was able to engage this woman in a dialogue that left her thinking that maybe it was, in fact, possible to be proud to be disabled.

A similar exchange took place when "My Voice My Turn" launched its bus campaign — called "What does normal really mean?" — which directed people to the website proudtobedisabled.com. A woman with a disability posted a message in our guest book at that website. She was quite angry and stated that she was disabled and was definitely not proud to be disabled and who did we think we were putting up such offensive information? Again, Thomas responded to this woman and posted a message to our guest book. He proclaimed that he was proud to be disabled and that his disability was a large part of who he was.

Patricia Okahashi, Action Hall ally, tells this story:

> Another member of the Hall has come a long way in the past ten years towards viewing his disability with pride. When I first met Lloyd, if handed a piece of paper, he would pretend to read it and so it was quite a few months before I realized he couldn't read. Today, he will often share that he can't read and that he has a learning disability if he feels safe enough. Lloyd and I both sit on the board of Homeless Awareness Calgary

Committee (HACC) and we were asked to write a short paragraph about ourselves for HACC's annual general report. Lloyd and I talked about what he wanted to put in his paragraph. I asked him if he wanted to put that he had a disability. Lloyd said that years ago, he would not have wanted to but now he feels okay putting that he has a disability. I asked Lloyd if he wanted to say that he was proud to be disabled. Lloyd said that he is not proud of being disabled, but maybe he should say that as a way to become more proud of being disabled. And so we included in Lloyd's biography that he had a disability and that he was learning to be proud of it because his disability is a big part of who he is.

Maintaining pride and a community of strength requires constant attention. As a group existing for over ten years, we will continue to struggle with identity, mental health and energy. Our work is never done — nor may we see the impact of our efforts come to fruition until years from now. It is critical that we spend a great deal of time nurturing activists and continue to create safe places for the work to continue. This takes us back to our story about Brodie. As one of our members commented,

When we started talking "pride" some people stood up and said: "I have nothing to be proud of, I'm a disabled person." Now they're saying: "We need a louder and prouder rally in March, because we're louder and we're prouder."

It has taken this group over ten years to create this sense of community, sense of pride and culture.

It is our dream that the Disability Pride Movement will help break down the barriers across economic and ethnic communities that are impacted by discrimination and income issues. We hope our work on building community, identity and a safe place will be a positive example for groups taking action with discrimination, citizenship, affordable housing and income disparity. We believe building movements on positive work such as disability pride and culture may engage marginalized groups and activists who have had difficulty building movements based on shame, and instead help build these communities based on diversity and common strengths.

Recently, a women's group has consulted with the Disability Action Hall on how they might structure their women's rights group and how we can learn from each other and complement one another's efforts. Fittingly, this group has named themselves "The Women's Action Hall" and we hope we can work together in the future.

If we neglect the cultural aspects of our movement, we will fail. There's only so far you can get with intellectual ideas, or even political clout. If you don't have your people fed and charged up, liking who they are and liking each other, wanting to stand by each other, you will fail. (Gill 1994: 49)

We hope that in sharing this chapter with other groups, we all can learn from each other.

Websites

<www.proudtobedisabled.com>
<www.ptff.org>
<www.actionhall.ca>

5

ALBERTA COLLEGE OF SOCIAL WORKERS

DOING THE RIGHT THING

Rod Adachi and Lori Sigurdson

> It's the action, not the fruit of the action, that's important. You have to do the right thing. It may not be in your power, may not be in your time, that there'll be any fruit. But that doesn't mean you stop doing the right thing. You may never know what results come from your action. But if you do nothing, there will be no result. (Mahatma Gandhi)

The Alberta College of Social Workers (ACSW) is the regulatory body for the profession of social work in Alberta. Social work is one of thirty professions governed by Alberta's *Health Professions Act* that obligates professional colleges to carry out regulatory activities that serve and protect the public interest. All social workers in the province must be registered with the College.

ACSW also represents the social work profession within Alberta. We support membership activities that promote skilled and ethical social work practice and advocate for policies, programs and services that serve the public interest. Our advocacy function gives social workers a voice where it matters for vulnerable peoples and communities across the province. Through our own campaigns and by partnering with others on social justice initiatives, the College can be the voice of the social work profession — helping all of us "do the right thing."

Mandatory Registration: Protection of the Public and Social Justice Advocacy

---

Know what your target is. Know very clearly. I mean — "mandatory registration" — that's all we needed to say and everybody knew what it meant. Very clear. "We want mandatory registration. We want to be part of the Health Professions Act." Focus. Don't give up. Find people you can influence and influence those who make decisions. Stay on target. (ACSW member)

Our work to achieve mandatory registration of social workers in Alberta was an advocacy campaign in and of itself. Achieving this legislative milestone was the result of a well thought out, focused effort that spanned several years. We began working on mandatory registration strategically in about 1990, with intensive efforts between 2000 and 2003. Luckily, social workers are accustomed to adversity, so we didn't give up half way through. Here's how one ACSW member who was part of the campaign described it:

We were not getting a lot of support… but we didn't let up and ACSW Council made a commitment and renewed the commitment again and again. We renewed the commitment to fight for better legislation. We just kept working on it.

It took a long time for our work to bear fruit. The end result was worth it — ACSW is now six thousand members strong. Other professionals, employers, clients and the general public know that we are educated, trained and accountable for our practice. Our inclusion in the *Health Professions Act* in 2003 increased public recognition of social work as a self-regulated profession and enhanced the College's credibility as a critic of social policy. For example, we are increasingly invited to give input on a variety of issues by government, media and organizations. According to one ACSW member, "through our own organization, ACSW, social workers should be able to achieve what our discipline has asked us to achieve." Most importantly, mandatory registration enables ACSW to play a significant social justice advocacy role in our province. Canadian and international social work codes of ethics specify the professional obligation of social workers to address issues of social justice. The legal requirement for social workers to be registered means that they must have "signed on" to the values and ethics of the profession, thus creating enormous potential for the mobilization of the six thousand-strong force of Alberta social workers. As one member put it, "when we got mandatory registration in Alberta — that was such a significant milestone for our profession." Another remarked, "I think having mandatory registration has given us more power and ability to influence change."

> When we got mandatory registration in Alberta — that was such a significant milestone for our profession. (ACSW member)

ACSW and Advocacy Activities

> Social workers, working together through ACSW, can in fact do things that they individually may feel uncomfortable doing. (ACSW member)

Every social worker has a professional commitment to address issues of social justice — but many are without the means to fully express this commitment in their working lives. For example, immersion in the day-to-day obligations of protecting children, counselling women leaving abusive relationships or providing homecare for older persons can leave workers with little opportunity to tackle the systemic issues they know create the problems in the first place. The advocacy function of ACSW affords each of its members the means by which to work to contribute to social justice work. We do this through a variety of approaches to advocacy that include our own initiatives, working collaboratively with other organizations and providing support for external activities.

ACSW Initiatives

ACSW's independent initiatives have included three major campaigns: the "No More Service Cuts" campaign (2001–2002); the "Raise Income Support Rates" campaign (2001–2003); and the "Closing the Disparity Gap" campaign (2008–present).

In 2001, we launched the "No More Service Cuts" campaign in response to government funding cuts that significantly impacted services to children. Cuts to Alberta Children's Services meant reducing services for children in need at a time when demand for services had increased by nine percent. The "No More Service Cuts" campaign involved newspaper ads, billboards, mailings to members and website postings.

We wanted the "Raise Income Support Rates" campaign to highlight the meager rates for income support programs. The ACSW campaign involved television and newspaper ads, a billboard campaign, website postings, information packages e-mailed to members of the provincial legislature and numerous meetings with government leaders and officials.

If these two campaigns were evaluated only in terms of whether or not the goals were fully achieved, neither would be judged very successful. The Children's Services budget was not significantly affected and there weren't big increases in income rates. But we think there are other important ways to think about success. In the quote that opens this chapter, Gandhi talks about how important it is to "do the right thing" even if you may not immediately see the results. The campaigns attracted attention that resulted in a heightened profile for ACSW among the public and stakeholders. People became more aware that we stood for children's rights and for fair income rates. The government recognized that ACSW represented a strong voice for poverty reduction. This recognition led to invitations to participate in a range of discussions on a variety of topics related to social justice.

ACSW is currently involved in the "Closing the Disparity Gap" campaign. The first phase of this "Disparity" campaign was an independent initiative of ACSW. In its later phases, the campaign has evolved to become more and more something we're doing in partnership with others. Here's how two of our members described the need for this campaign:

> One of the problems in this province over the last five or ten years is the growing income disparity of the benefits that have come from the oil boom in the tar sands. The benefits have gone to 40% of the Albertans. 60% have made no gains. And if you look at the data about how income is distributed, Alberta has the wealthiest people in Canada, and also the poorest. And the gap between the two is growing.

> Certainly Alberta is booming economically, but we've left behind the social piece. And there are a lot of Albertans who are vulnerable and marginalized, who aren't benefiting and require better services and programs. So we hope to bring some balance through our work, through our "Disparity" campaign.

Through the "Disparity" campaign we hope to:

- Gain adoption by the Alberta Government of a social policy framework that commits to closing the disparity gap through an integrated approach to delivering social programs (that is, an enhanced awareness of the link between private troubles and public issues). The disparity gap refers to the economic and social distance between the richest and poorest households.
- Continue to raise awareness of Alberta's income disparity gap and the impact it has on social work and social work's client population (provide a voice for the voiceless).
- Increase member engagement (build power through membership).
- Create an environment in Alberta that results in social workers being valued, appreciated and respected.

This has been one of ACSW's biggest initiatives to date. We phased the first part of the campaign to coincide with the 2008 Alberta election. One of our strategies was producing and posting interviews of social workers on our website. These podcast interviews identified the challenges social workers and their clients were facing in several fields of practice such as child welfare, family violence and settlement services. We developed handbills and distributed them to all social workers in Alberta to encourage their participation in the campaign to reduce the disparity gap. Through the handbills, social workers were invited to ask candidates questions that were relevant to our profession. Candidate responses were then posted on our website in order to inform voters of their views on social issues. Our goal was to broaden the discourse during the election. Along with their focus on the economy — and especially the oil and gas industry in Alberta — we believe social issues should be a key focus for politicians.

Collaborating with Other Organizations

In 2003, ACSW started an initiative called "Influencing Social Policy and Development" to support collaborative activities with other groups. We recognized the progressive work of other organizations that are promoting the public good through collective responsibility. As social workers we strongly believe in the pursuit of social justice. The Canadian Association of Social Workers (2005) Code of Ethics states, "Social workers promote social fairness and the equitable distribution of resources, and act to reduce barriers and expand choice for all persons, with special regard for those who are marginalized, disadvantaged, vulnerable and/or have exceptional needs." Working with other groups makes all of us stronger, increasing our ability to achieve this ethical responsibility. As one ACSW member put it,

> Through networking and through coalitions we're able to do more. And then, other groups have different networks, different ways of getting their message out, so it expands the audience. So I think you have to do both. There are things that you have to take the lead on, because somebody has to do it. And if you think that's very important, you must do it. But on the other hand, there are some areas where there are many stakeholders... so why don't we work with them and maybe that's the best way to do it.

ACSW now has formal partnerships with six organizations. These partnerships take varying forms. ACSW is a founding member of both the Parkland Institute and Public Interest Alberta. We have been a longstanding organizational supporter of the Friends of Medicare, the Edmonton Social Planning Council and the Alberta Alliance on Mental Illness and Mental Health. Recently, ACSW became a member of the Greater Edmonton Alliance. In addition to providing financial support through annual fees, the ACSW promotes the activities of these organizations and usually has a representative serving on their respective governance boards.

A recent example of collaborative work involves another part of the "Disparity" campaign called the "Who Cares Alberta?" initiative. ACSW worked with nine other organizations: Alberta Association of Services for Children and Families; Alberta Council of Women's Shelters; Alberta Community Council on HIV; Alberta Council of Disability Services; Alberta Home Visitation Network Association Boys and Girls Clubs of Alberta;

Canadian Outcomes Research Institute; Child and Youth Care Association of Alberta; and Public Interest Alberta. Together we used strategies that educated the public regarding the issues through media releases, the development of videos that examine the challenges of caregivers and a postcard distribution campaign to the Premier of Alberta (see Figure 5.1). The "Who Cares Alberta?" campaign highlighted the human resource crisis — community social service agencies were

ACSW file photo

having difficulty recruiting and retaining staff due to low wages. We think the campaign resulted in greater recognition of the issue and minor budget increases. In November 2007 the Provincial Government announced $26.1 million in funding to support the retention and recruitment crisis in human service agencies.

All of ACSW's initiatives are about "doing the right thing." Even if no changes are immediately visible from this work, it is still important to do it. You're left with the status quo if you do nothing, which isn't an option for social workers committed to social justice goals. Speaking out about concerns gives hope to clients, social workers and other professionals. Whether or not the results are measureable, we are having an impact on issues. Encouraging a broader analysis of issues, broadening the discourse, is significant in itself. As social workers we recognize the right and ethical obligation of our members to participate in professional and community associations in order to influence the development of social policies. As Gandhi says, "if we do nothing there will be no result."

Supporting Others' Advocacy

A third approach to advocacy involves providing support to external activities in the form of financial donations and/or promotions. ACSW has been able to set aside a limited budget from which donations can be provided to support events and activities such as the Alberta Social Forum and a recent conference on homelessness in Calgary. Through these kinds of contributions, ACSW is able to support the progressive work of others. Our limited resources mean that we are unable to take the lead on all social problems. However, ACSW can contribute through financial and networking support to other agencies and activities.

Albertans were encouraged to send the above post card to Premier Stelmach to show support for the "Who Cares Alberta?" campaign.

The ACSW Social Action/Social Justice Committee

One way members can be directly involved in ACSW's advocacy activities is through membership on the Social Action/Social Justice Committee. This committee is a recent development that has historical roots; ACSW previously had a committee working on social action. Currently, the committee has twenty members. They have identified three levels of advocacy activity that reflect ACSW's past actions: major ACSW-driven initiatives on a provincial scale; working collaboratively with other advocacy groups; and supporting regional activities. The committee meets monthly and is focusing on the "Closing the Disparity Gap" campaign. The key work currently is developing social work leadership. On March 19, 2010 at the ACSW Annual Conference we launched our social policy framework for Alberta. This framework, entitled "Visioning a More Equitable and Just Alberta," is an advocacy tool for social workers and stakeholders to use in promoting progressive social policies that support publicly delivered programs and services that are accountable to Albertans (such as affordable housing, family supports and services for the disabled). Relationship development with members of the provincial legislature and other key political officials by social workers is underway.

Reflections on What We've Learned

Advocacy campaigns have little power if those running them do not have credibility. Our achievement of mandatory registration increased our power and therefore enhanced all future advocacy activities. (ACSW member)

One specific advocacy activity impacts all the others. The cumulative impact of our advocacy efforts is becoming more apparent. Increasingly we are being included in advisory capacities, sought out by the media and identified as an important stakeholder on various fronts. This increases our power to influence based on our values as social workers. It is now recognized that "if there are issues of social relevance, social work is called upon as a profession to have input" (ACSW member).

At ACSW, we've learned that there is value in adopting multi-faceted strategies in our advocacy efforts. Some of what we've learned:

- It's important for us to have a Social Action/Social Justice Committee. The committee helps us maintain momentum in our advocacy efforts.
- Relationship building through collaborative initiatives helps to build critical mass.
- Advocacy activities raise the profile of the organization, which leads to greater recognition and invitations to be a voice at the table.
- Advocacy work helps individual social workers get involved in social justice efforts, which creates momentum.
- Advocacy requires time, effort and patience.

Mandatory registration enables ACSW to play a significant social justice advocacy role in our province. (ACSW member)

We see our actions gain momentum, which gives us energy to face challenges that remain. Lingering worries about ACSW's regulatory function may influence some members' involvement. Even greater challenges to membership engagement are structural — in Alberta, the dominant political culture doesn't give much encouragement to progressive voices, and the province's longstanding conservative government has given rise to bureaucratic inertia and resistance to change. In this context, alternative points of view are dismissed or even denigrated. In good social work style, we try to see opportunities in the challenges. Whereas in more varied political environments, social justice advocacy groups may become splintered, our context creates potential for unifying opposing voices. As ACSW becomes increasingly recognized as a profession under the *Health Professions Act*, its external power grows and the social work voice becomes stronger. As the social work voice becomes stronger, our social justice advocacy activities can bear more and more fruit, which will increasingly engage our members. We create momentum though stronger voices and increased membership engagement unified in our work toward social justice. We've learned that successful advocacy takes time and effort, but we're patient — because we know it is the right thing to do.

or conferences. When the issues are familiar to us we decide quite quickly whether or not to become involved. Our participation usually depends on having sufficient members able to attend the event. We always try to join activities planned by the organizers of International Women's Day. We join with like-minded activists from all over the city and are seldom the only activist group at an event.

Our projects are not like those of most groups represented at the Calgary symposium. For us, a large project is a forty-five minute program for a one-time occasion. To demonstrate, we'll describe different gigs.

The Year of the Older Person

Where have all the doilies gone
That seniors used to make?
Where have all the cosies gone
Long time ago?
Seniors are so active now
Have no time to age right now
Too young for rocking chairs
Or an-ti-ma-ca-a-sers.
(To the tune of "Where Have All the Flowers Gone?")

The year after the Calgary Raging Grannies organized, the United Nations declared 1999 as the Year of Older Persons. This helped us focus on one objective: to challenge society on its views of older people (especially women) as having outlived our usefulness. We wrote songs and we borrowed them from other Gaggles. We modeled an alternative: older women aware of the issues and bent on doing something about them, and willing to be a bit outrageous for a good cause. One song that we wrote asked "Where have all the doilies gone?" and concludes, "We have grey power, we voice opinions, protesting when we find the need."

Another song goes: "My grandmother's heart got a new valve repair and it gave her a new lease on life" (see "My Grandmother's Heart" in the Appendix at the end of this chapter). We performed these songs and others about seniors (see "Geriatric Sexpot" in the Appendix) at an afternoon showcase in Calgary's Devonian Gardens and we continue to sing them at seniors' centres around town.

We feel we're effective when people both old and young respond with surprise and pleasure at seeing us. We've made presentations in schools, such as high school Social Studies classes on democracy and in post-secondary Women's Studies courses on aging. One Mount Royal College course on Women and Aging was especially satisfying, as students' comments showed relief that aging needn't mean doddering away into invisibility.

A variety of gigs followed the Year of the Older Person. At one event we performed in front of 100-200 people, which was a very successful gig. Other times we sang to pedestrian traffic, particularly when we were picketing a place. As one of our members commented,

> If we picket something like Wal-Mart or another consumerist place, many people will… walk by with their eyes averted… but if you get into a conversation with somebody, sometimes a penny will drop, so that is a different feeling of success.

The Pride Rainbow Project

In 2005, we demonstrated with the Pride Rainbow Project. This action was in organized by five teenagers at the Unitarian Church of Calgary who wanted to draw attention to the right and need of same-sex partners to marry legally. The teens sewed a huge banner of rainbow colours which eventually grew to five hundred feet. We helped carry the first ninety feet of their rainbow banner at the Gay Pride parade. We helped again when they organized the official launch of the banner. For that evening, we wrote and sang a number of songs. We were invited to sing one at a press conference at the Unitarian Church of Calgary the next day. There, a group of seven leaders from different faith groups responded to Bill 38, the civil marriage bill. That had us featured on the evening CBC National News with quotes from the speakers, plus a short clip from our song "Going to the Chapel" (see the Appendix). We knew we were successful, for the audience spontaneously joined us on the chorus.

Just days before the bill that supported same-sex marriage passed, our teenage friends took the Rainbow Pride Banner to Ottawa, displaying the five-hundred-foot length near Parliament Hill. They led the way and we supported them. We can't take credit for the bill passing, but we are proud of our part in drawing attention to the widespread support for it. When a law is changed, we know our combined action has been effective.

Getting media coverage is a huge indicator of success to us. Coverage on national television was and is great, but we also welcome local and provincial television coverage. One of our Grannies was interviewed after an action at Paul Martin's Liberal Party breakfast at Stampede Park. She was featured at length on the television news that evening, making our case and begging Martin not to sign the missile defence treaty, which was being debated in parliament at the time. Many times the press has put our issues and our pictures in the newspaper or on television.

Protest at the CAPP Convention

In May 2008 we joined other activist groups during the Canadian Association of Petroleum Producers (CAPP) convention in Calgary. There, we demon-

strated with activists from B.C. and Alberta, including one of the Edmonton
Raging Grannies. Several speakers, about half of them Aboriginal, spoke
about the effects of the oil sands industry on land, water, wildlife and air.
We learned a lot from the other speakers, appreciating the challenges of
northern Aboriginals in a new way. We sang a song called "Five Hundred
Ducks" (see the Appendix).

What made this action effective was our partnership with other groups,
excellent media coverage and the location at the entrance to the CAPP convention, a pedestrian walkway in the heart of the city. Most of the audience
consisted of lunch-goers and passers-by. We were a little audacious, receiving
many laughs in one verse:

> Syncrude spinners tried to pass the buck,
> Blaming Mother Nature and their bad luck.
> But who can deny an oil-soaked duck.
> Boo to Syncrude! Do they give a — (seal lips)
> (To the tune of "Six Little Ducks")

We think it's really important to show our support to those primarily affected by this industry, and we want to add the perspective of older
middle-class women. In order to strengthen our credibility, we try to write
lyrics based on solid research. We try to simplify the facts and the content
into something that is understandable, accurate and sits well with us. It's a
challenge getting our research right. However, the political announcements
of the following weeks, describing the government's intentions to monitor
and control the environmental impacts of oil-sands development, show just
how relevant our song and our presence were at the time. We also continue
to hope that the grand general statements of the government plan will result
in specific details, financing, timelines and consequences for failure to adhere
to new regulations. To that end we will continue to protest and act.

How Do We Know When We Are Effective?

Sometimes it's simply the look on the faces of the people in the audience. In
a demonstration urging City Council to eliminate pesticide use for cosmetic
purposes, the discomfort on the face of a certain Alderman who had a vested
interest in pesticide use showed we got our point across. Also, we knew we
were successful when a young man at a shopping mall stopped and talked
with us. He would never have thought about the anti-consumerist message
of Buy Nothing Day if we hadn't been there. He did, though, so that felt
good. We definitely work to get the point across.

Audience response also tells us if we're effective. Some people were angry
and indignant that we were at Paul Martin's Stampede Breakfast. This was

shortly after his successful election, when he invited his local volunteers to a breakfast. We protested the cruise missile pact and waved little missiles in their faces. Security told us we had to leave. So we did, slowly, singing all the way down the line-up of people waiting to enter the pavilion. Some of the people cheered and waved, so there was support as well as official criticism. Obviously, not all Liberal volunteers were in favour of acting with the U.S. on cruise missile testing and use. We made our point and people listened.

Many people who hear us must have similar beliefs to ours, because they are attending the rallies. We sing what others are thinking and encourage them to take action, which may be in the form of sending letters, signing petitions or meeting with politicians. We may do that as individuals, and our songs tell others they are not alone.

We know we're successful when there's participation by the general public. One of our members commented:

> On the G8 demonstrations sidelines there were many locals and friends on bicycles or pushing baby buggles... We had been warned that [the protests] may turn violent, and it was a concern because many of us in this city have jobs and connections and family in the oil business. What would happen if we were arrested? Yet, the first thing we saw at Eau Claire Market, [the scene of one of the protests], was local police in spandex on bicycles. Reaching mainstream people is a huge success.

What Do We Think Facilitates Our Effectiveness?

We do not back down. We have to persevere in presenting our point of view and our opinions — perhaps that is just being stubborn. We were proud when our former Premier Ralph Klein said he would have made more progress in privatizing Medicare if it hadn't been for the Friends of Medicare and the Raging Grannies. One of our favourite songs for rallies opposing the privatization of health care is "In My Weakened Years," to the tune "When I'm 64" (see the Appendix).

These are factors that make us effective:

- We don't back away from controversy. We sing opinions that we know disagree with conventional practice. We can say what we think. We take pride in telling our politicians what to do, trying to skewer them on the spit of their own comments when possible.
- We are outrageous as we try for attention. A member of our Gaggle cannot be afraid to make a fool of herself in public for a good cause. Maybe at her first gig a Granny will feel that way, but the experience usually takes away the fear. If a Granny isn't comfortable with public action, there are many other ways to be an activist.
- We are colourful and photographable. Our Granny clothes, shawls, hats and boots make us easily identifiable to protestors, media and potential members.

- We provide sound bites for media coverage. We present our point of view through singing and humour. We try not to be sarcastic or satirical, because then people might not understand our intent. We try to be straightforward, leaving little to misinterpretation. Whether coverage is television, radio or print, we present something pithy on the issue.
- We have strong networks. We are almost always working with another organization. We attended a gig with the Disability Action Hall to attract media attention to their cause. That was true at the CAPP convention as well.
- We support others who initiate actions. In the words of one of our members,

> Once a group organized a rally at McDougall Centre, [the provincial offices in Calgary], and when we arrived there were two of their people, six of us and one policeman. We managed to convert the policeman to our point of view.

In an opposite circumstance, at the G8 rally, "we joined with thousands of protestors [including other Raging Grannies from B.C., Saskatchewan and Alberta]." According to one Granny, "that was much more effective because there were so many people involved. It was a huge event here in Calgary. The march was covered for the numbers that came out and for the variety of the people who were part of that." Another Granny said,

> We were part of it, and I'm proud. It was lots of fun and very exciting... Each of us alone can do tiny little bits, and that is what Grannies do... By pulling all the groups together, you've got a thousand times more power than any one of us by ourselves. You got to be part of this network... We sing to support the people who are in the frontlines and working in particular areas.

- We publicize our willingness to support the underdog. In spring of 2008 we organized a public rally to show support for young children at risk. When the Salvation Army closed the Links and Bridges Program, which they had been running for children, they did so with very short notice. As a consequence, nothing was in place for the pre-schoolers, for there were no comparable programs. We were angry because of how the Salvation Army handled the situation. Because we wanted to find some way to honour the staff and parents of the children in Links and Bridges Program, we organized a rally. These children were definitely underdogs. We wrote letters, advertised well and had a pretty good turnout at the rally. What made it effective was working with the staff and parents at Links and Bridges. At the rally, parents talked about what the program meant to them. Psychologists talked about the program's impact and stressed the importance of early intervention for children. It was a very satisfying event.
- Our events are non-violent. The following comments were offered by Grannies who attended demonstrations during the week of the G8 meeting near Calgary.

At the G8 rallies it was wonderful to be part of such an incredible event. We would encourage the group and be on the sidelines. I remember holding the sign and yelling and it felt just so wonderful. They were so appreciative of us, and so loving toward us. It was nice. It wasn't just a radical fringe. There was no violence.

The police department infiltrated us and cheated. But maybe that was good, because they learned that we didn't want violence… if the police had come down on them hard, I don't know what would have happened. You can't control a whole group of young, excitable people, who are mad as hell.

- We do what isn't expected from older women. At Paul Martin's breakfast, "we were all quite excited because… this was the first real political thing that we had done independently." And "We felt like we were being bad little girls, which was quite helpful… It was fun to be silly and a little audacious, and to go where we weren't wanted."
- We collaborate with other generations, as evident in these comments:

Because I'm an old person, and most of the others at the G8 rallies were very young, it was so positive, so uplifting to meet those young people, which I normally wouldn't have come into contact with. As I met them and became more aware of who they were, and what they were trying to do, and what their intentions were for the G8, I just thought they were wonderful young people. I would leave every meeting feeling just positive about the world.

It's young people that are largely engaged in these things, and they are easily dismissed by the establishment. So if they can get the Raging Grannies involved they feel as though it's not as easy to dismiss what they are about. So weird as we may look, we are in fact older, supposedly wiser women and if we're engaged in their issue, it helps to give it some credibility.

It also may make it safer for them, because we are older and we are watching how the protestors are being treated: "We use our status as mature women, surprising people with the topics and the words and the things that people don't expect old ladies to do." And: "We have a rap song, and when we sing it we put baseball caps on and turn them backwards."
- We prepare carefully.

I was at the university meetings to plan for [the G8], then I just invited the Grannies to be involved… Each of us was contributing in whatever way we could to get the information out there… lots of work [in advance] with the police… practice songs for a couple of weeks, planned our meeting place, we all knew our words, even though we carry our words with us. We don't rely on memory.

- We are not accountable to anyone else for funding. We are not accountable to anyone except ourselves. We meet rent-free at the Unitarian Church, where five of our Gaggle attend. We've heard about the effect of funding on other groups. Not being funded gives us the gift of freedom. We don't really have to worry about who might limit what we want to do.

What Are Our Aspirations?

Our aspirations go along with challenges that accompany those dreams. We want to have more members. We need more members to revitalize the group and share the responsibilities. We don't know how long we can keep the group vibrant with the challenges from our aging bodies and dwindling energy. Like some of our favourite causes, it's about sustainability. How do we keep ourselves and our group healthy and active? It's important that we respect each other when one of us has to take time out because of health or family concerns. We've held two recruitment parties in the last two years but attendance of newcomers has been small.

Another aspiration is to be better performers, to have more dramatic impact and possibly include choreography. Perhaps we could develop street theatre at some point. However, that would require a lot of practice time. Each of us has a busy life, committed to other volunteer action in churches or community groups, pursuing art or writing or part-time paid work. So far we are not able to put the time into practicing dance moves or skits. On the other hand, we need to remind ourselves that we are social and political activists, not entertainers. It has to be enough that we do what we do, in the way we do it. We don't have to do everything. There are others who can and will present the same message in more polished ways.

An aspiration we identified a few years ago was to do more spontaneous intervention, just to pop up, instead of relying on someone else to organize an event. We've gone to malls on Buy Nothing Day to tell the shoppers why they shouldn't be there. We have been escorted out several times. We also sang alternative Christmas carols about poverty and war toys, on Stephen Avenue Mall.

> What's most important to us is getting our messages across to people who we think might learn from them. Sometimes if we're close to pedestrian traffic, we focus on one verse of one song. We might have handbills to give to passers-by. Sometimes we pick one verse that encapsulates the issue and our passion, singing it over and over.

We do enjoy supporting like-minded people. We need encouragement as well and get that from other activists. Although we may target CAPP or other large institutions, we also will go out to support a group that needs more media attention.

We need to ensure we're not perceived just as entertainers. Our purpose is to be social activists, not amusement.

We risk running ourselves too thin, which is another challenge because, as you've read, there are so many causes that drive us. Spreading ourselves so thin makes it hard to be informed enough to write lyrics that are relevant and thought provoking.

> If you're knowledgeable about something and you really know how it happens [then we share it]. If you don't know, then you find out. We go to websites and we contact people who do know. We look at the studies and we share them.

Almost all of us have gone through several years of academic study, and we know how to research.

> If we need more information before we can make a decision, then we find out before the next meeting… This doesn't happen very often, because we've all taken it upon ourselves to become as informed as possible, in many different areas. We all read extensively. We share what we know via email, from different organizations to which we belong. Sometimes there's a lot of reading between meetings.

Another challenge is to be able to respond quickly. Sometimes we've pulled our group together in a couple of days. Most of the time, however, we need to plan two weeks ahead. We need time to prepare, time to practice and time to present.

Being in the right place at the right time is really important. That's where our networking helps. We need to know what other groups are doing and we are on many activist e-mail lists.

How Has Our Work Been Successful? Well, How Do We Measure It?

It's different every year. Sometimes we measure success by media coverage. It may be a picture in the corner of a magazine cover, for example the November 2008 issue of *Alberta Views*. There was a time when we were considered very effective at targeting politicians. The Edmonton Raging Grannies are a strong presence at the Provincial Legislature Building, informing themselves and others of issues.

Getting change in legislation is one way to measure effectiveness, but it's also effective to just have our say.

> We can say what we want and respond to many programs to get a public reaction. We sometimes get put down or criticized. A former Granny, who moved to Victoria, was appalled at the negative reaction of her new neighbours regarding the Victoria Grannies. I think that's a point in [our] favour.

Another way we know we're effective is a changed political stance after we send letters to MLAs and MPs.

What else makes a big difference is people saying "Oh, I saw the Grannies and I'm glad you're doing this." We get a lot of encouragement from others, often shy or very busy people who would not do this themselves.

Another measure of success is being original and committed to being different. Groups need to develop their own signature and style. Our songs are designed to be singable, using tunes familiar to the audience. "If people can understand us, because we have articulated the words well, than that is a success." If they nod in agreement or laugh at the right times, that's a big measure of success.

Another way we know we are successful is if we are having fun. It's too draining to do this work if it's not fun. We all like to sing. We all value the camaraderie of our gigs. We all like each other as people and women. It's so important to be around people who are excited about what they are doing. As one Granny put it, "We're always having fun. That energizes you. You go to a meeting and when you come out of it you're energized, you're not exhausted." And another: "One time we wound up as the opening act for Bishop Fred Henry... We thought it was very funny... he seemed a little quizzical himself."

What sustains us is the fun, but also the awareness that we're part of a huge movement. We are not alone. "We feel we are making a difference. We feel empowered as individuals, because we are part of a small group that has found a fun way to state our opinions."

> Feelings of success come [from being] part of something that is bigger than yourself... to work with other people with similar ideas, and to be out there. You just have to believe in the kinds of things that we do and not be afraid to make a fool of yourself.

Not many organizations offer that.

Our advice is to network, network, network. When you spend time with other groups, get on their e-mail lists. Exchange contact information through business cards and brochures. Help your effort to multiply, repeat and prevail. Support each other by advertising and attending each other's events. When we get the information on issues we care about, we try to follow up with letters or phone calls. It's more effective if these come from somebody not aligned with the affected group. For letters and phone calls we usually identify ourselves as individuals, not as members of the Raging Grannies.

Knowing ways to attract media coverage is very useful. Writing good press releases is vital when planning an action. We agree to advertise our presence on posters or press releases that others prepare. We can help in supporting events that others plan. Even if a rally or march doesn't draw many people, if there's a media person or two in attendance the event is more likely to get coverage with the Grannies present. That's how our costumes, songs and signs help. One sign says, "If you think you're too small to be effective, you've never been in bed with a mosquito." We have a big sign saying who we are, but also have little signs on which we can easily change the text.

The last thought we will share with you is that we all need to believe in ourselves and our actions, even if it feels like we're spitting into a heavy wind:

"It's empowering to be part of doing something for others. It is incredibly empowering and important."

Keep at it.

Appendix: Raging Granny Songs

My Grandmother's Heart

Tune: "My Grandfather's Clock" (Calgary Raging Grannies, Spring 1999)

My Grandmother's heart got a new valve repair
And it gave her a new lease on life.
She had lived through war, the Depression a-and more
Led her family through endless strife.

Too-oo active for life in the o-old rocking chair
She wanted to change the-e score
So she JUMPED - UP - determined to go again
Grabbed her dancing shoes -
Raced out the door.

Ah-One-Two-Ah-One-Two-Three-Four

Tune: "In the Mood"
(Calgary Raging Grannies, Spring 1999)

She just stared rockin' and she wouldn't give up
She just keeps on movin' - she don't know when to stop
Outdances all the me-en who are ha-alf her age
Keeps the party groovin' - she is qui-ite the rage
We just can't believe it - she-e can't get enough
Keep it going granny 'cause we like your stuff!

In the groove - oh yea - That's my granny
In the groove - mmm - She's off her fanny
In the groove - uh-huh - She's feeling dandy
She's slippin', she's slidin', she's exercisin'!

If you want to meet a - *real* cool cat...
Come see *granny* (stage whisper)
Come see *granny*
Come see *granny*
She's - *where it's at.*

The Geriatric Sexpot (or Sex… eeeh!)
Tune: "There'll Always Be an England" (Raging Grannies, origin unknown)

I'm Sixty and I'm Sexy
At least that's what I hear
From the programs seen on TV
And the talk shows on the air.
The magazines print articles
By some Authority
All telling me, at sixty,
I'm as Sexy as can be!

I'm Seventy and Sensual
Though it really doesn't show
Geriatric experts tell me
I'm mature and all aglow.
They say hidden wells of passion
Are just bubbling up in me
And at seventy I've hit my peak
Of sensuality!

I'm Eighty and I "Ought to"
There's no time to put things off
No excuses like, "I'm breathless"
Or "Exertion makes me cough".
For I'm told I've still got fires
That I didn't know I had
And I would tell my husband but
When I wake him, he gets mad!

Now I'm Ninety and I'm Naughty
Ant there's nothing new to me
I've been having sex since sixty
And I'm tired as can be.
But I'm telling you a secret
And it's one that you must keep
When I get to be One Hundred
I am darn well going to sleep!

Going to the Chapel
(Granny Sharon, Calgary Raging Grannies, April 2005)

Bells do ring. Laws do pass.
Gays have won more rights at last.
They cause no harm as they sing their love song.
With the marriage law they know they belong!

Chorus:
So they'll be going to the chapel
And they're gonna get married.
Oh, they're going to the chapel
And they're gonna get mar-ar-aried.
Gee it makes them happy
Just to know they have the chance
To honour a lifetime of love.

Marriage has changed through centuries past.
Spouse has gained equal property at last.
Marriage provides a spouse with that right
And protection from others who fight.

Chorus.

Let's raise a toast to this bride and groom,
Or are they partners? Do we have room
To stretch out our minds and definitions too
And allow them to live like me and you?

Chorus.

To those who say that gay love is wrong
We know that justice is moving along.
Lesbians and gays we now recognize
That their love is equal in our eyes

Five Hundred Ducks

Tune: "Six Little Ducks"
(Granny Sharon, Written for CAPP conference, June 16, 2008)

Five hundred ducks on the tailings pond
Tried really hard but they couldn't fly on,
Cause their feathers were encrusted with an awful guck,
Boo to Syncrude! Love a duck!

Premier Stelmach tried to pretend
His plan for the environment was good to the end,
But the ducks told the truth, for they were stuck.
Boo to Syncrude! Love a duck!

500 ducks is what they said
Turns out 1600 were dead
They drowned and sank into the muck
Boo to Syncrude! Love a duck!

Syncrude spinners tried to pass the buck,
Blaming Mother Nature and their bad luck.
But who can deny an oil-soaked duck.
Boo to Syncrude! Do they give a ---(seal lips)---

Boo to Syncrude! Boo to Syncrude!
Boo to Syncrude and love a duck!

In My Weakened Years
Tune: "When I'm 64"
(Calgary Raging Grannies, for FAIRE Rally September 25, 2004)

Now that I'm older, losing my health,
In my weakened years…
Will I still be counting on my family's care?
Or nursing home, oh patient beware!
If I'm in need of twenty-four-seven
Will they treat me fine?
Will they show caring,
Always forbearing,
When I'm eighty-nine?

I could be hurting, managed by pills,
Not making any sense.
Will there be enough staff to take care of me?
And will their training help them to see
That I'm still an elder
Trying to live
With some dignity.
Will they have patience
With all their patients
When I'm ninety-three?

Alberta's surplus, dear Mister Klein,
Can change our future now.
Let's establish standards so we all can be
Living well in health and safety.
As I grow older, losing so much,
Facing many fears.
How will they treat me?
Please don't defeat me
In my weakened years.

7

THE PEMBINA INSTITUTE

ALBERTA'S OIL SANDS ROYALTY REGIME – THINKING LIKE OWNERS

Marlo Raynolds and Amy Taylor

The Pembina Institute[1] was founded in the mid 1980s in the small rural Albertan town of Drayton Valley after one of Canada's most significant industrial accidents — the Lodgepole sour gas blowout.[2] A group of concerned citizens established the organization to help prevent such an accident from happening again and to ensure that the most appropriate approaches to oil and gas developments were being pursued from environmental, social and economic perspectives.

Now, twenty-five years later, the Pembina Institute is a nationally recognized think tank of sixty professionals focused on energy and environment issues in Canada. Pembina's mission is to advance sustainable energy solutions through innovative research, education, consulting and advocacy. The organization's three top priorities are: realizing major reductions in the environmental impact of the oil sands; advancing greenhouse gas reduction policies across Canada; and helping Canada take advantage of its massive renewable energy resources in an appropriate way.

In pursuit of our priority to reduce the impact of the oil sands, in 2005 the Pembina Institute began a multi-year effort to update the fiscal (royalty and tax) regime applicable to Alberta's oil sands. The regime, having been established to spur oil sands development at a time when fuel prices were low and the cost of oil sands production was high, was out of date and in need of reform. Instead of capturing maximum revenue for Albertans, the owners of the oil sands resource, the low royalty rates and generous tax breaks provided by the provincial and federal governments put corporate interests ahead of citizens interests and facilitated an unsustainable boom in development.

It was for these reasons that we began encouraging Albertans to "Think Like Owners" and insist that their government, the manager of their oil sands resource, maximize revenue collection from developments. This is a David versus Goliath story of a small group of under-resourced people tackling a huge industrial complex on a significant injustice to Albertans. This story shows what a dedicated team can accomplish but also the realities of the challenges when standing in opposition to multi-billion dollar companies.

The Campaign Part 1: Drawing Attention to the Issue

Alberta's oil sands resources are owned by the citizens of the province. (Pembina member)

In Alberta, the vast majority of non-renewable resources, including oil sands resources, are owned by the citizens of the province.[3] The Department of Energy manages the publicly owned oil sands resources on behalf of the citizens.[4] In its role as resource manager, the government allows companies to acquire rights to develop the oil sands resource. These companies incur development costs and if they are successful and produce oil, they also receive revenue from its sale. The government is responsible for ensuring that an appropriate portion of the revenue from the sale of the oil goes to the citizens of Alberta as the owners of the resource.

Governments around the world use royalties to collect revenue from the extraction and sale of non-renewable resources. This is true in Alberta as well where the government collects revenue from oil sands developments. Royalties require companies to pay the government a specified percentage of the revenue they earn on the sale of the oil resource. The royalty rates need to ensure that the companies retain a fair return on their investment and that other revenues are returned to the citizens of the province. When governments set royalties too low or offer significant royalty breaks (credits, exemptions, rebates), the government is short-changing the rightful owners of the resource and companies get more than their fair share.

The Pembina Institute has done oil sands-related work for many years. Historically, our focus has been on identifying, communicating and putting forward solutions for the negative environmental impacts associated with oil sands developments. However, in 2005 we identified what we felt was a significant injustice with respect to the royalty rates companies operating in the oil sands were paying to the citizens of Alberta. Between and 1997 and 2005, world oil prices more than doubled and production of the oil sands, spurred on by low provincial royalty rates, increased by eighty-eight percent. Amazingly, during the same time period, Albertans, the owners of the oil sand resource, saw their share of this economic boom in the form of royalty revenue decline for each barrel of oil from the oil sands. Albertans received $2.85 in royalties for each barrel of oil sands oil in 1997 and only $1.74 in 2005 — this, at a time of record-breaking profits for the industry.

Alberta's Oil Sands Royalty Regime

Alberta's oil sands are subject to the provincial Oil Sands Royalty Regulation, commonly referred to as the "generic royalty regime." The regime was implemented in 1997 following recommendations of the National Task Force on Oil Sands Strategies[5] that were released in the spring of 1995. In 1993 the Alberta Chamber of Resources convened the National Task Force on Oil Sands Strategies, a collective of oil industry and government representatives who drafted a framework that would create the conditions necessary to make the oil sands an economically attractive resource. The Government of Alberta had a number of objectives in mind when it developed and implemented the royalty regime (Masson and Remillard 1996):

- Accelerate the development of the oil sands.
- Facilitate development of the oil sands by private sector companies.
- Ensure that oil sands development is competitive with other petroleum development opportunities on a world scale.

In essence, the regime was designed to overcome barriers related to high capital costs[6] and encourage the large investments needed to develop the oil sands resources by collecting minimal royalties until developers have recovered their costs (Mitchell, Anderson, Kaga and Eliot 1998). To that end, the regime imposed a twenty-five percent royalty on net project revenue after the developer has recovered all project costs, including one hundred percent of capital, operating and development costs in the year incurred, and after the corporation had earned a rate of return on its investment equal to the Government of Canada Long-term Bond Rate. In the event that these conditions were not met, for example when investments were high due to project start-up or expansion, the project owner paid a minimum one percent royalty on all project production (Pigeon 2003).

The twenty-five percent royalty on net project revenues applicable to the oil sands is a "resource rent royalty" — a royalty levied on the economic rent, the net revenues associated with a project. "Ad valorem royalties" (such as those applied to natural gas and conventional oil in Alberta) are based on gross revenues and do not take costs into consideration. Because resource rent royalties take costs into consideration, we would expect them to be set higher than ad valorem royalties.

Resource rent royalties, if properly established, provide a means to transfer a precise and consistent share of economic rent from corporations undertaking developments back to citizens. However, in the case of Alberta's oil sands, the resource rent royalty rate for oil sands (twenty-five percent of net revenue) was set below the ad valorem rate that applies to conventional oil (up to forty percent of gross revenue) and natural gas (up to thirty-five percent of gross revenue) in the province. Thus the twenty-five percent royalty rate put corporate interests ahead of citizens' interest.

Indeed, this exceedingly low royalty rate meant that companies operating in the oil sands were reaping excess profits at the expense of the real owners of the resource — Albertans. The low royalty rate meant that not only were Albertans being short-changed for the development of their resource, but the pace of development that was occurring in the province may have been faster than would have been the case under a regime which maximized revenue collection for resource owners as companies sought to take advantage of low rates.

Exposing the Oil Sands Injustice

With sufficient evidence to indicate that Albertans were not getting their fair share from oil sands developments in the province, the Pembina Institute set out early in 2006 to make oil sands royalty reform an issue that Albertans would care about. The first task was to let people know that, in fact, they, not the companies undertaking the developments, were the owners of this valuable resource. The second hurdle was to demonstrate that, as owners, they were not getting their fair share; that the royalty rates were out of date and needed to be reformed to reflect the current economic reality. While the low rates may have been justified in the past when costs were higher and fuel prices lower, that was no longer the case. We proceeded to release a series of reports, op-eds and fact sheets on the subject of resource ownership and fair share providing evidence of low royalty rates for oil sands in Alberta. We made a number of presentations and did numerous media interviews on the subject to bring the issue to light in Alberta. We worked with other organizations and individuals with an interest in the subject.

Collectively, we were successful. While government may have been satisfied with the status quo, it was clear that Albertans were not. Research polls early in 2007 showed that sixty-one percent of Albertans supported reforming the oil sand royalty regime so that Albertans obtained a greater proportion of revenues. With the Alberta public on side and clear evidence of the injustice of the current regime on hand, royalty reform became an issue that was not going to go away easily. Indeed, it soon became a key issue in the leadership race that took place in the fall of 2006. While the premier at the time, Ralph Klein, had no interest in royalty reform, candidates for his replacement agreed during their campaigning to undertake a royalty review should they be elected.

Asked to clear the matter up yesterday, Premier Klein couldn't even confirm if the review Melchin [Alberta Minister of Energy] talked about had been done. "I don't know if it was completed or not, nor do I give a tinker's damn whether it was completed or not." *(Calgary Sun 2006)*

The Campaign Part 2: From Review Announcement to Panel Report

On December 3, 2006, Ed Stelmach became Premier of Alberta. Since he had previously committed to conducting a review of royalties in the province, our focus shifted from making royalty reform an issue to influencing how royalty reform should occur. We are convinced that the Pembina Institute played a critical role in getting royalty reform recognized as an issue in Alberta. Our reports, fact sheets, presentations, media work and collaboration with individuals and organizations helped make Albertans aware of the issue, which contributed to the announcement by government that policy action would take place.

A Blueprint for Royalty Reform

It was now time to turn our focus to the process for royalty reform. Given the complexity of the topic, we felt that it would be difficult for lay persons to engage in the review to any great depth. Yet, given that Albertans are the owners of the oil sands resource, in our opinion it was critical that the review be conducted by them and for them. It was for these reasons that the Pembina Institute recommended that a citizens' assembly be held through which Albertans, chosen at random, could become educated on royalty systems and make recommendations on reform for Alberta. The citizens'

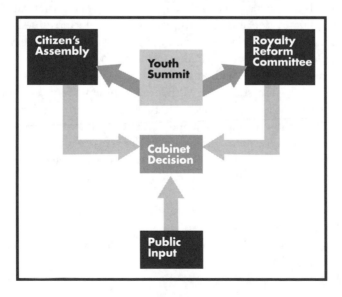

assembly would take place in parallel to an expert royalty reform committee as well as other avenues for broad public engagement (for example public hearings or on-line submission forms). An opportunity for youth to engage in the review was also seen as vital for the process to be a success. A schematic of our recommended royalty review process is presented below.

At the time the review was announced, we were not resourced or equipped to recommend exact numbers for royalty reform. We had focused on the inadequacy of the current regime and the need to update it but had not made specific recommendations on what the new rates should be. We continued with our strategy by focusing our recommendations on an appropriate process to get at the right royalty structure. It was for all Albertans, as resource owners, to decide. Furthermore, to put a number out there would provide too much of a target for our adversaries to shoot down and make us look unreasonable; the solution should come from all Albertans.

Unfortunately, despite direct lobbying efforts with the new government and some favourable traction amongst a few key bureaucrats, the government did not choose to pursue a citizens' assembly. Our assumption on why it did not happen is that it was seen as too complicated and risky for a risk adverse new government. The process was moving forward quickly and unfortunately we did not have the time or resources needed to adequately convince the government that a citizen's assembly was the way to go. We were no longer setting the agenda or the timing; the government was forging ahead with the review process with little consideration for process.

Alberta's Royalty Review Process

In February 2007 the Provincial Government announced that it had assigned an expert panel to review the royalty rates (and tax treatment) not just for Alberta's oil sands but for conventional oil and natural gas as well. Public hearings on the matter began in April with the panel's final report due to be delivered at the end of summer. We had to quickly turn to preparing a submission to a process we felt was inadequate.

As per the terms of reference set by the Government for the review process, the expert panel held meetings in five locations throughout the province. Stakeholders and interested Albertans were invited to attend a meeting in one of the five locations to make a presentation to the panel. Albertans were also invited to provide comments online.

The Pembina Institute committed to making a presentation when the panel was in Calgary in mid-May. We decided that, at that time, we would release a report identifying and describing a series of options for royalty reform for the oil sands. We held a press conference in the same building as the panel meetings and released our report just prior to presenting our findings to the panel. We limited our recommendations to ways in which the oil sands royalty regime should or could be reformed to get a better deal for

Albertans.[7] It was here that we felt the greatest injustice to Albertans was occurring and here where we chose to focus our limited time and resources.

However, while we made an explicit decision to limit our recommendations for reform to oil sands, we did not communicate this decision broadly within the oil and gas sector. Thus, the perception that prevailed was one of Pembina versus all oil and gas. We may have been perceived quite differently if we had clearly singled out the oil sands or if, furthermore, we had tried to align in support of natural gas and conventional oil as a way of placing additional pressure on the oil sands. Instead, we had the conventional oil and natural gas folks pitted against us as well as oil sands companies. Collectively, they launched anti-reform websites; there were more corporate jets in Calgary than ever seen before; and they hired some of the most powerful public relations firms in the country. Given more time, or had we seen this move coming, we could have reached out to the conventional oil and gas companies and tried to get them on our side or at least not have them opposing us to the degree that they did.

The Campaign Part 3: Read the Report

The Royalty Review Panel concluded that Albertans were not getting their fair share from the development of their oil and gas resources. (Pembina member)

On September 18, 2007 the final report of the Royalty Review Panel, "Our Fair Share," was made public. After about seven months of research, analysis and input, the Panel concluded that Albertans were not receiving their fair share from energy developments and that, in fact, they hadn't been receiving their fair share for quite some time. According to the Panel, "The royalty rates and formulas have not kept pace with changes in the resource base and world energy markets" (Alberta Royalty Review Panel 2007: 4). The Panel went on to say that the onus was on the Alberta Government to re-balance the royalty and tax system so that a fair share is collected. To that end, the Panel made a number of recommendations for reforming Alberta's energy royalties to update the outdated royalty regimes for oil, oil sands and natural gas. The recommendations were designed so that Albertans would retain a greater share of revenues from the development of their resources while maintaining Alberta's competitive advantage among world energy investment opportunities. The outcome of the Panel's work confirmed the analysis we had made and the injustice we had worked to expose.

Following the release of the Panel's report, the Pembina Institute launched the "Read the Report" campaign. The idea of the campaign was to draw Albertans' attention to the report of the Panel. The conclusions were clearly of great significance to all Albertans and we felt it was important that Albertans be made aware of what the government-appointed Panel had concluded. We circulated a letter from the Chair of the Panel as well as a link to the report to as many relevant organizations as possible in Alberta. We conducted extensive media on the Panel's report and encouraged all Albertans to read it. We provided a summary of the report on our website. Our objective was to have the report speak for itself. The recommendations were based on solid research and analysis. It was our hope that the recommendations would be taken as a package and implemented as soon as possible.

Reflections on the Change Strategy
Expose the Injustice

The starting point in the change strategy for our royalty reform work was not much different from that of many of our other campaigns. More specifically, we felt that if we exposed the truth and the injustice that people would understand that they were getting short-changed and would thus demand change. We think that the strategy worked. We chose a frame ("Think Like Owners") that worked for Albertans and we presented the numbers that clearly demonstrated that Albertans were losing out while corporations made record profits. The injustice was exposed. People understood that their resource manager, the Government of Alberta, was not capturing their fair share of revenue from the development of their oil sands resource.

Framing and Communications

A critical part of our success was the framing and communications strategy corresponding to our work in this area. We identified the "Thinking Like an Owner" frame early in our work and used it consistently over the course of the four years in which we were heavily engaged in this work. For Albertans to care, it was critical that they first understand that we were talking about their resource; that they were the owners and, as owners, they had to hold their manager, the Government of Alberta, accountable. Our choice of language and framing was critical, especially in the Alberta context, where there is an aversion to government and a belief in heavy reliance on the free market. We could not use any kind of frame that evoked "government taking more money from private companies." Instead we chose to focus on Albertans "thinking like owners." This was about government management, about managing the resource all Albertans owned in an appropriate and efficient manner. In the four years of this work, we consistently used this frame and we believe it was successful given the adoption of "fair share" language and the fact that the royalty review process happened at all.

Doing a Lot With a Little

The Pembina Institute had very limited resources for taking on the royalty issue in Alberta. Indeed, our "Thinking Like an Owner" campaign is a prime example of a relatively successful campaign delivered with minimum funds and staff. An initial grant from a foundation allowed us to write the first "Thinking Like an Owner" report. This report was critical in bringing the injustice of the current royalty regime to light in the province. With the initial grant used up, however, we found it increasingly difficult to secure funds to support our oil sand royalty work. Corporations were clearly not interested in funding such work and it was a topic that, as a rule, foundations were able to grasp and comfortably support. With the help of senior staff we were nonetheless able to continue to piece sufficient funds together to remain at the forefront of the issue for a number of years. The generous support of past donors, who were called upon to come to our aid, meant that we could keep staff driving the issue forward in Alberta and participating in the review process and follow up as needed.

Robust Tactical Work

The Pembina Institute first highlighted the low royalty rates applicable to oil sands in the 2005 publication "Oil Sands Fever: The Environmental Implications of Canada's Oil Sands Rush." In 2006 we did a more in-depth analysis of the extent to which the low royalty rates were shortchanging Albertans, and published a paper dedicated to the topic called, "Thinking Like an Owner: Overhauling the Royalty and Tax Treatment of Alberta's Oil Sands." The paper provided evidence of low royalty rates and declining take for resource owners in the context of high fuel prices, reduced industry costs and record breaking profits for companies operating in the oil sands.

Over the course of 2006 Pembina staff were quoted in the media on a regular basis and made numerous presentations on the topic of oil sands royalty reform. In the fall of 2006 when a leadership race was called in Alberta, we made royalty reform a key issue and all of the key candidates committed to a review of the royalty rates should they win the election. In February of 2007 we released a blueprint for royalty reform in which we made recommendations on how to conduct a formal review of the royalty regime. Later that same month the Provincial Government announced that an expert panel was assigned the task of making recommendations on reform to the Government of Alberta. In the months that followed, Pembina staff prepared their submission to the expert panel.

In May 2007, the Pembina Institute held a press conference to release "Royalty Reform Solutions," which described several ways in which the oil sands royalty regime could be reformed to ensure maximum revenue for citizens while maintaining the viability of oil sands projects. Concurrent with the release of the report, Pembina staff made a presentation to the Panel.

Reports and media are important parts of any change strategy, but on their own they are insufficient. Thus, in addition to numerous reports and significant media, we undertook a number of lobbying activities. We worked with usual and unusual allies to push for the royalty review and boost participation in the review itself. We wrote a number of op-eds and made presentations at every possible opportunity.

Lessons Learned

Following the release of the Royalty Review Panel report, the Government began back-pedaling on royalty reform. They undertook closed door consultations with industry and made comments in the media implying that they would not be implementing the full suite of recommendations put forward by the Panel. In October they released "The New Royalty Framework" which described the changes they intended to introduce, including changes to the oil sands royalty regime. The Government announced that the twenty-five percent royalty on net income applicable to oil sands companies would increase for every dollar oil is priced above $55 per barrel, and to forty percent when oil is priced at $120 or higher. The change was less of an increase than what we had asked for in our presentation to the Panel, and was less than the Panel had recommended the Government pursue. It was nonetheless a step in the right direction.

We have identified the following lessons from our experience campaigning for royalty reform in Alberta:

- The combination of solid research and a powerful frame with dedicated outreach was a significant contributor to the success of our campaign.
- Another key factor was being able to take advantage of a political opportunity, namely the lead-up to the leadership race in the province.
- It is critical to be able to quickly react to changes in timelines. We were so entrenched in the mode of pushing to draw attention to the royalty injustice in the oil sands, that when the Government announced that a review process would be launched so quickly after the election we were somewhat caught off guard. We were no longer setting the timeframe and we needed to quickly change our thinking to how best to engage and have an effect on the process the Government would be driving forward.
- Because we were initially so focused on drawing attention to the oil sands royalty issue, we hadn't taken the time to think through our entire campaign. Therefore, we did not have our "Blueprint for Royalty Reform" already prepared and in the waiting for when a review was announced. By the time we got the blueprint out the door, the timeframe was too tight to have any real influence on the government process. They were

skeptical of the citizen's assembly idea, and it was largely dismissed before careful consideration. Had we released it earlier, or built it into the original campaign, there would have been more time for us to try to gain traction on it and a greater potential for it to be adopted. We believe that a citizens' assembly on royalty reform could have ultimately had a significant impact on the outcome of the review process.

• Choosing the right communications frame and sticking to it throughout the campaign was critical to our success. We chose a frame that spoke to Albertans and got at the heart of the injustice we were exposing. We used the same frame consistently and repeatedly over the course of four years.

• While we were explicit in our decision to put forward recommendations for reform focused solely on the oil sands, we did not consider trying to work with relevant actors in the conventional oil and natural gas sectors to get them more onside with our recommendations. We were thus seen as wanting changes not just to oil sands but to conventional oil and gas as well. Had we done a careful analysis of how to get the biggest bang for our buck, we may have chosen to speak out more in support of conventional oil and natural gas, which may have put increasing pressure on the oil sands where we wanted to see the biggest changes.

• When the Royalty Review Panel released their report, we were extremely impressed by the depth of their research and the rigour of their recommendations. We hoped that the report would speak for itself and that just getting Albertans to read the report would mean the recommendations would be adopted.

• In retrospect, because the oil sands recommendations put forward by the Panel were a bit less significant than those we had been calling for, we may have been better off pushing for bigger changes. If we had done so, we would have created a spectrum of changes for consideration from A, status quo, to C, the changes we wanted to see. If we pushed for C from A, we may have had a greater chance of getting B, the Panel's recommendations. In other words, by advocating for more extreme changes to the regime, the Panel's recommendations would have seemed more moderate and thus perhaps had a greater chance of being adopted.

Notes

1. More information on the Pembina Institute is available online at <pembina. org>.
2. Sour gas spilled at a rate of 150 million cubic feet per day and on some days the rotten egg odor could be smelled from as far away as Winnipeg.
3. A portion of oil and gas resources are privately (rather than publicly) owned. For privately owned resources, royalties are paid to individual landlords. This

chapter is concerned with publicly owned oil sands resources.

4.   Only 2.6 percent of the area covered by oil sands are privately owned. The rest are on public lands and, as such, are owned by all the citizens of the province (Alberta Energy, personal communication, September 2005).

5.   In 1993 the Alberta Chamber of Resources convened the National Task Force on Oil Sands Strategies, a collective of oil industry and government representatives who drafted a framework that would create the conditions necessary to make the oil sands an economically attractive resource.

6.   A typical oil sands mining and upgrading project that delivers 100,000 barrels of oil per day requires $4.5 billion in capital expenditure. This figure does not include typical capital investment overruns of fifteen percent (Mawdsley, Mikhareva and Tennison 2005).

7.   While we had released a paper in 2004 comparing Alberta's conventional oil and natural gas royalty rates with those of other regions (in Canada and elsewhere), since 2005 we had largely focused our royalty work on the oil sands.

8

Sheena Jamieson and Leighann Wichman

INTRODUCING OUR SUPER HEROES

THE BOARD OF DIRECTORS

THIS GROUP OF COMMUNITY LEADERS DEDICATE THEIR TIME AND EXPERTISE TO ENSURING THAT THE YOUTH PROJECT HAS THE RESOURCES IT NEEDS TO OPERATE. THIS TEAM HOLDS THE POWERS OF FUNDRAISING, PUBLIC RELATIONS AND THE LAW. BY DAY THEY ARE STUDENTS, LAWYERS, TEACHERS, FINANCIAL PLANNERS, PARENTS, SOCIAL WORKERS, AND OTHER NOBLE PROFESSIONS. BY NIGHT THEY ARE YOUTH PROJECT SUPERHEROES FIGHTING TO MAKE NOVA SCOTIA A BETTER PLACE FOR LGBT YOUTH.

THIS GROUP OF YOUTH LEADERS HOLD THE POWERS OF PROGRAMMING! THEY ARE RESPONSIBLE FOR ALL THE SERVICES AND PROGRAMS THAT ARE OFFERED AT THE YOUTH PROJECT. STEPPING IN TO PROVIDE A VOICE FOR YOUTH ACROSS THE

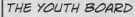

THE YOUTH BOARD

PROVINCE, OUR TEAM WORKS HARD TO GET THE JOB DONE. THEY WORK CLOSELY WITH THE STAFF TO ENSURE THAT THE YOUTH PROJECT OFFERS RELEVANT, USEFUL AND NEEDED SERVICES AND PROGRAMS. THEY WORK DILIGENTLY ALONG SIDE THE BOARD OF DIRECTORS. THEIR POWERS ARE EQUAL AND COMPLEMENTARY.

THE STAFF

THE STAFF AT THE YOUTH PROJECT CARRY OUT THE SERVICES AND PROGRAMS TO YOUTH ACROSS NOVA SCOTIA. THEY TRAVEL TO SCHOOLS AND COMMUNITIES ALL OVER THE PROVINCE PROVIDING SUPPORT, EDUCATION AND ADVOCACY. THE TIRELESS EFFORTS OF THE STAFF MEMBERS ENSURE THAT THE DAY-TO-DAY OPERATIONS OF THE YOUTH PROJECT RUN SMOOTHLY AND THAT LGBT YOUTH ISSUES ARE REPRESENTED IN ALL ASPECTS OF YOUTH LIVES, WHETHER THAT IS SCHOOLS, FAMILIES, COMMUNTITIES OR GOVERNMENT. THE CLOSEST PARTNER OF THE STAFF IS THE YOUTH BOARD. THESE TWO TEAMS WORK TOGTEHER TO GET THE JOB DONE!

WITHOUT A SIDEKICK TEAM OF DEDICATED VOLUNTEERS, THE YOUTH PROJECT WOULD BE LOST. OUR VOLUNTEERS PROVIDE ADDED SUPPORT

VOLUNTEERS

AND GUIDANCE TO YOUTH, SERVICES AND PROGRAMS. THEY ENSURE THAT THE GUIDELINES ARE FOLLOWED, EVERYONE IS COMFORTABLE, AND SAFE AND THEY ACT AS COMMUNITY ROLE MODELS. VOLNTEERS ARE VAULABLE MEMBERS OF THE YOUTH PROJECT TEAM!

THE YOUTH

THE YOUTH OF NOVA SCOTIA WHO ARE LESBIAN, GAY, BISEXUAL, TRANSGENDER, OR ALLIES ARE THE REASON THE YOUTH PROJECT EXISTS. THESE FEARLESS AND RESILIENT YOUNG PEOPLE ARE HEROES THEMSELVES. MANY OF THEM FIGHT FOR THEIR RIGHTS AND VOICE IN THEIR OWN SCHOOLS AND COMMUNITIES. OTHERS, CALL ON THE SUPPORT OF THE YOUTH PROJECT SUPERHEROES, AS THEY STRUGGLE WITH THE EFFECTS OF HOMOPHOBIA, TRANSPHOBIA AND HETEROSEXISM. THROUGH THE SUPPORT AND PROGRAMS AT THE YOUTH PROJECT MANY OF THESE YOUTH WILL BECOME PART OF THE SUPERHERO FAMILY. IT IS THE INTERESTS, NEEDS AND PARTICIPATION OF YOUTH THAT ALLOWS THE YOUTH PROJECT TO FLOURISH AND CONTINUE TO STRIVE TO REACH OUT TO YOUTH ACROSS NOVA SCOTIA. IT IS THE VOICE OF THE YOUTH THAT IS THE LOUDEST, STRONGEST AND HAS THE MOST IMPACT.

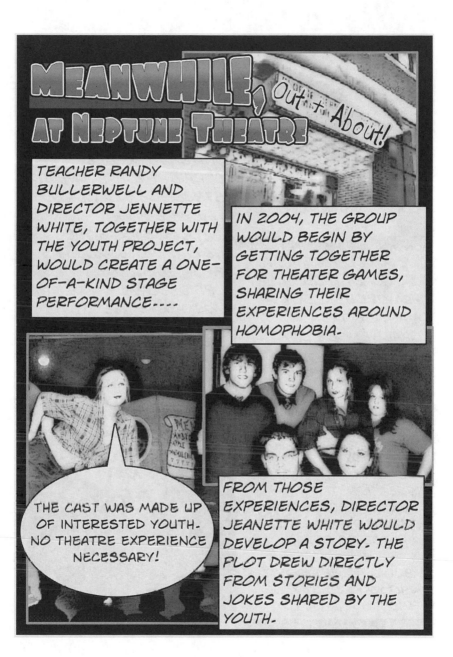

OUT & ABOUT!

WHY CAN'T I HOLD MY BOYFRIEND'S HAND IN PUBLIC?

THE PLOT OF "OUT & ABOUT" TAKES PLACE IN AN ALTERNATE UNIVERSE, WHERE STRAIGHT YOUTH HAVE TO STRUGGLE IN A WORLD WHERE BEING GAY/LESBIAN IS THE NORM. THE WORLD HAS BEEN TURNED UPSIDEDOWN – IT IS GAY YOUTH WHO ARE PRIVILEGED TO LIVE OPENLY, WHEREAS STRAIGHT YOUTH ARE FORCED TO HIDE WHO THEY ARE.

WE AIMED TO TAKE A CRITICAL, THOUGH HUMOROUS, LOOK AT MANY OF THE CHALLENGES GAY, LESBIAN AND BISEXUAL YOUTH FACE:

*STEREOTYPES

*THE EFFECTS OF HOMOPHOBIA (LONELINESS, ISOLATION, THE CHALLENGES OF COMING OUT TO OTHERS, FINDING A PLACE TO FIT IN)

*BEING ACCEPTED FOR WHO YOU ARE BY YOUR FRIENDS AND FAMILY

BE WHO YOU ARE!

THE REASONS FOR THE SUCCESS OF THE PLAY INCLUDE...

YOUTH VOICE

IT WAS WRITTEN BY LGBT YOUTH!

YOUTH DIRECTION HAS ALWAYS BEEN ONE OF THE PRIMARY GOALS OF THE YOUTH PROJECT. IT WAS IMPORTANT TO US THAT "OUT & ABOUT" WAS GUIDED BY YOUTH SHARING THEIR OWN EXPERIENCES INSTEAD OF OTHERS SPEAKING FOR THEM.

STRONG PARTNERSHIPS!

IT WAS EXTREMELY HELPFUL TO FIND PEOPLE WITH STRENGTHS IN AREAS WHERE WE LACKED EXPERIENCE, SUCH AS DIRECTING AND THEATRE.

THE DEDICATION FROM OUR SUPPORTERS AND DIRECTORS, CAST, YOUTH PROJECT STAFF, NEPTUNE THEATRE AND OTHERS ENSURED THAT EVEYONE CARED ABOUT ITS SUCCESS

IT DELIVERED A STRONG MESSAGE

A PLAY WAS THE PERFECT FORMAT TO DELIVER A DIRECT AND IMMEDIATE MESSAGE. WITH A LIVE AUDIENCE IN FRONT OF US, WE COULD GIVE A PERFORMANCE AND HAVE A DIRECT CONNECTION TO OUR VIEWERS.

IT WAS CREATIVE

IN CONTRAST TO OUR USUAL INK AND PAPER RESOURCES, A PLAY OFFERED A NEW WAY TO SPEAK TO OTHERS USING REAL PEOPLE. OUR AUDIENCE WAS ABLE TO REACH OUT TO US AFTERWARD AND INTERACT WITH THE CAST AND CREW.

IT WAS FUN

THERE WERE MANY LONG HOURS BUT A LOT OF LAUGHTER!

THE PLAY WOULD
DEBUT AT THE
ATLANTIC FRINGE
FESTIVAL TO POSITIVE
NEWSPAPER REVIEWS.
AS ENCOURAGING
FEEDBACK KEPT
COMING IN,
EXCITEMENT ABOUT
THE PLAY CONTINUED
TO GROW. THE YOUTH
PROJECT'S
SUPPORTERS,
FUNDERS AND ALLIES
WERE EXCITED TO SEE
WHAT WE COULD DO.

"OUT & ABOUT" WOULD
EVENTUALLY MAKE THE
FESTIVAL'S HIT LIST
FOR SELLING THE
MOST TICKETS AT OUR
VENUE AND EARNED A
GLOWING REVIEW IN
THE PAPER.

LESSONS WE HAVE LEARNED...

HAVE FUN

MAKE WHATEVER YOU'RE DOING AS FUN AS IT CAN BE.

IF IT ISN'T FUN, YOUTH PROBABLY WON'T WANT TO DO IT.

PATIENCE

CHANGE IS SLOW, AND IT'S HARD TO SEE IT IN DAY-TO-DAY EVENTS. IT'S NOT A SPRINT — IT'S A MARATHON.

PERSISTENCE

OBSTACLES ARE INEVITABLE, BUT NOT IMPOSSIBLE.
EVEN IF THEY ARE SYSTEMIC ISSUES, IT IS POSSIBLE TO MAKE A SMALL IMPACT. LOTS OF SMALL IMPACTS CAN MAKE A LARGE ONE.

PARTNERSHIPS ARE IMPORTANT!

MANY OF THE GREAT THINGS WE HAVE DONE HAVE HAPPENED THROUGH PARTNERING WITH OTHER ORGANIZATIONS AND PEOPLE

BY COLLABORATING WITH OUR ALLIES, WE HAVE BEEN ABLE TO CREATE MORE EFFECTIVE EVENTS AND BUILD NEW RELATIONSHIPS.

THE IMPORTANCE OF YOUTH DIRECTION

TO ALWAYS RECOGNIZE THE VALUE OF LISTENING TO AND INCLUDING LGBT YOUTH IN YOUTH PROJECT DECISIONS AND OPERATIONS.

TO ALLOW YOUTH TO TAKE ON LEADERSHIP AND DECISION-MAKING ROLES, AND FACILITATE A YOUTH-DRIVEN ENVIRONMENT.

AS THE STORY CONTINUES OUR HEROES FACE MANY CHALLENGES...

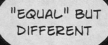

POLITICAL CLIMATE

EACH NEW GOVERNMENT SETS THEIR OWN PRIORITY AREAS AND MAINTAINS, DISCONTINUES OR CREATES NEW FUNDING PROGRAMS. A POLITICAL CLIMATE THAT SEES SEXUAL ORIENTATION AND GENDER IDENTITY ISSUES AS A LOW PRIORITY OR AS LESS THAN EQUAL IN SOME AREAS WILL MAKE IT DIFFICULT TO GATHER

"EQUAL" BUT DIFFERENT

RELIGIOUS INTOLERANCE

I RUIN RELIGION FOR OTHERS

RELIGIOUS INTOLERENCE IS NOT ONLY A THREAT TO EQUALITY, BUT IT ISOLATES MANY YOUNG LGBT PEOPLE FROM THEIR FAMILIES AND COMMUNTITIES. ON TOP OF THAT, THOSE WHO USE RELIGION TO SPREAD HATRED AND IGNORANCE MAKE IT DIFFICULT FOR SUPPORTIVE RELIGIOUS PEOPLE AND GROUPS TO SHOW THEIR SUPPORT TO LGBT PEOPLE.

CONTINUED FUNDING

SHOW ME THE MONEY

MANY FUNDING SOURCES REQUIRE THAT MONIES BE ATTACHED TO A NEW PROJECT WHICH DOES LITTLE TO HELP MAINTAIN EXISTING PROGRAMS AND ACTUALLY ADDS NEW WORK ONTO THE ALREADY OVERLOADED HEROES AT THE YOUTH PROJECT. ENSURING THERE IS FUNDING TO OPERATE ON A DAY-TO-DAY LEVEL, WHICH INCLUDES STAFFING, UTILITIES, AND TRAVEL IS THE BIGGEST CHALLENGE IN THE FUNDING ARENA.

SLOW MOVING SYSTEMIC CHANGE

WHILE MANY CHANGES CAN BE SEEN, SUCH AS THE EMERGENCE OF GAY STRAIGHT ALLIANCES AND YOUTH HEALTH CENTRES, THE SYSTEM REMAINS SLOW TO ADAPT. THERE IS STILL NO CHANGE TO THE CURRICULUM, HOMOPHOBIA IS STILL RAMPANT IN SCHOOL HALLWAYS AND TRANSGENDER STUDENTS STILL STRUGGLE TO FIT IN TO A BI-GENDERED SYSTEM THAT IGNORES THEM OR DENIES THEM.

IGNORANCE AND APATHY

THERE ARE STILL MANY WHO BELIEVE SOME OF THE MYTHS AND STEREOTYPES THAT EXIST AND MANY OTHERS WHO ARE UNAWARE OF THE ISSUES AND CHALLENGES FACED BY LGBT YOUTH. AS A RESULT, LGBT ISSUES ARE STILL OFTEN LEFT OUT OF NEW INITIATIVES, POLICY DEVELOPMENT AND RESOURCE EXPANSIONS.

A FOCUS ON QUANTITATIVE VALUES

GOVERNMENTS AND FUNDERS STILL RELY HEAVILY ON STATISTICAL DATA. THEY WANT TO KNOW HOW MANY AND HOW MUCH. WORKING WITH MARGINALIZED POPULATIONS, WE KNOW THAT SOME THINGS JUST AREN'T THAT EASY TO MEASURE. THIS RELIANCE ON NUMBERS CAN LEAVE THESE GROUPS OUT IN THE COLD AND CERTAINLY NOT ON THE TOP OF A PRIORITY LIST!

1,2,3,4,5...

LEADING LIVES AS HEROES CAN BE TIME CONSUMING AND CHALLENGING AS A YOUNG PERSON. ADULT ATTITUDES, BUSY LIVES, AND ACCESSIBILITY MAKE OUR HEROES WEARY. MANY YOUTH HAVE PART TIME JOBS, DON'T HAVE ACCESS TO TRANSPORTATION OR DON'T KNOW HOW TO ACCESS SUPPORT. THERE ARE A LOT OF COMPETING PRESSURES IN THE LIVES OF YOUTH. YOUTH WITHOUT PARENTAL SUPPORT CAN FIND IT EVEN MORE CHALLENGING

THE YOUTH PROJECT'S HOPES FOR THE FUTURE ARE:

WE HOPE TO BE ABLE TO CONTINUE TO EVOLVE AND ADAPT IN ORDER TO MEET THE CHANGING NEEDS OF LGBT YOUTH. WE SEE THIS AS A LONG-TERM GOAL WITH MANY STAGES AND STEPS. WE DON'T WANT TO BECOME OBSOLETE BECAUSE WE ARE NO LONGER MEETING CHANGING NEEDS.

IMMORTALITY ... MWA HA HA

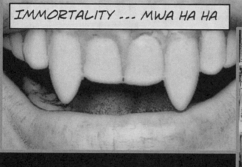

1993 – FOREVER

YOUTH DIRECTION

IT IS VITAL THAT YOUTH HAVE POWER AND CONTROL WITHIN THE YOUTH PROJECT. THIS WILL KEEP US RELEVANT AND HELP US EVOLVE. WE WANT A FUTURE WHERE THAT CONTINUES TO BE VALUED AND A PRIORITY.

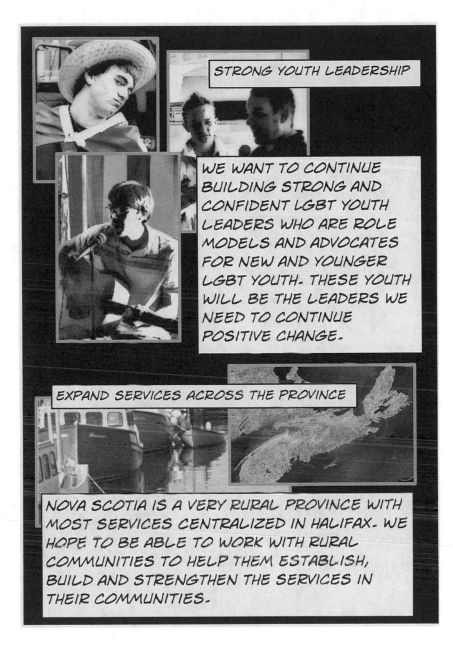

STRONG YOUTH LEADERSHIP

WE WANT TO CONTINUE BUILDING STRONG AND CONFIDENT LGBT YOUTH LEADERS WHO ARE ROLE MODELS AND ADVOCATES FOR NEW AND YOUNGER LGBT YOUTH. THESE YOUTH WILL BE THE LEADERS WE NEED TO CONTINUE POSITIVE CHANGE.

EXPAND SERVICES ACROSS THE PROVINCE

NOVA SCOTIA IS A VERY RURAL PROVINCE WITH MOST SERVICES CENTRALIZED IN HALIFAX. WE HOPE TO BE ABLE TO WORK WITH RURAL COMMUNITIES TO HELP THEM ESTABLISH, BUILD AND STRENGTHEN THE SERVICES IN THEIR COMMUNITIES.

9

SOCIAL JUSTICE COMMITTEE

SUCCESS IN RECRUITING
AND RETAINING VOLUNTEERS

Derek MacCuish and Maria Rasouli

> I started to become quite concerned about the way the world was going and felt that I needed to do something positive, to make a positive contribution in the world... [Social Justice Committee is] a type of organization that gives you the capacity to get involved to what ever level you wish to be involved.[1]

In 1975, a small group of Montrealers gathered in a church basement to see if they could find ways to show their solidarity with the social movements fighting oppression in Central America. They called themselves a "social justice committee" and began setting up discussion evenings and hosting guest speakers. As the years went by, the group saw that the need for education and advocacy on human rights was not diminishing. So it evolved, taking on more issues and formalizing its role in society by becoming a registered charity — The Social Justice Committee of Montreal (SJC). In the 1990s, the SJC went global in focus, taking on issues related to Third World debt, globalization and the international financial institutions — the World Bank and International Monetary Fund (IMF). Often, the work on Central America is linked strongly with the global issues. For example, we successfully campaigned for Canada to cancel debt payments by Honduras after the country was badly damaged by Hurricane Mitch. The inequalities in Central America continue to be a focus, along with the broader context of global finance.

Today, our areas of work continue to be public education and policy advocacy, and we still fight for the protection of human rights defenders in Central America, reform of global financial institutions and, more recently, corporate social responsibility. The SJC is now recognized internationally as a lead organization for debt cancellation and for greater accountability, transparency and democratic processes in the world's main financial institutions, the World Bank and IMF.

Our audience has also widened. When the SJC was formed, the target was English-speaking Montreal. Now, of the thirty or forty workshops we present each year, half are in French. Our magazine, the *Upstream Journal*, has evolved from a newsletter for our donating members to a magazine with national distribution.

These days, the SJC runs a wide range of programs along with the educational workshops. We've hosted conferences and film festivals and our theatre program is going strong after more than ten years. The resource materials we provide, in print and via the internet, to high school students and teachers are in use throughout the province of Quebec. It's hard to believe we do this with only two full-time staff.

A volunteer staffs an information table as participants gather for a panel discussion of corporate social responsibility in impoverished countries. Teams of trained SJC volunteers lead about fifty workshops every year, in both English and French. SJC file photo

How Do We Do All This With So Few Staff?

The truth is that our work relies almost entirely on our volunteers and interns. At the SJC, our effectiveness depends on our volunteers, who devote time and energy to work on Third World poverty — which isn't interesting for everyone — and do it from a distance. Montreal is a long way from Liberia or Guatemala and we don't run concrete development projects such as digging wells or building schools.

Our volunteers and interns are dedicated, highly motivated and capable. They are eager to learn, have a strong sense of ethics and reflect an exceptional level of awareness and responsibility. They value the potential knowledge and skills they can acquire from volunteering with us. Many of our volunteers are students or recent graduates at the beginning of their careers. Other organizations seem to struggle to attract and motivate volunteers. At the SJC, we are fortunate to have many who are engaged every day in all aspects of our education and advocacy work. And every day we get more e-mails from individuals asking how they can get involved. It's empowering for us to see how much the areas in which the SJC works resonate with the public. One person described the wide range of roles available to the SJC volunteers as follows:

> In terms of what you do as a volunteer in the organization, well of course you can be part of the Board of Directors, which is involved in decision making issues… you can be involved in fund raising… you can be involved in doing the education work, such as I do, and in organizing events. You can wind up doing office tasks, like some of the people in the other room are doing. You can be doing media work, in which you try to get involved with the media and encourage the media to follow these issues. We have our own newsletter, so you can be involved in creating articles and doing the editing for the newsletter. We have a theatre troupe, which does street theatre and dinner theatre.

How Did Our Volunteer Program Emerge?

For many years we did not have a strong volunteer base and relied more on staff to do the work. At that time, staff regarded volunteers as people who provided support, doing the small tasks that allowed the staff to implement programs. Volunteer involvement was sporadic and was linked to the fluctuations in how much we needed their help.

Over time, the demands on the organization changed and intensified. We've expanded our areas of focus, developed new educational materials, and put a lot of effort into ensuring services are provided in both English and French. Our workshops are increasingly popular; we've raised the bar on production quality and distribution of the magazine and taken on more ambitious events such as organizing bigger conferences. Our office environment, too, has changed. We now have a dozen networked computer stations, with high-speed internet and the software needed for a range of tasks, from managing the accounting to designing a poster.

> If it's not done by the volunteers, with the guidance of staff, it won't happen. So I think that keeps people involved, although it's hard as well, because it demands a lot when you're involved.

To meet the changed demands, the SJC needed to take a new approach and give volunteers more responsibility. We needed to craft a cohesive volunteer program with defined volunteer roles. We also needed to establish a process for recruiting, selecting and training volunteers. We now have an application process to assess candidates' suitability and to see if their interests match the SJC's work. Applicants complete a form or give us a resume — we look at their education and employment background and areas of interest. We then schedule a half-hour interview, during which the candidate meets a staff person so we can get to know each other a bit to determine the person's interests and capacities and how they fit our needs.

Based on a personal experience, I would say that the Social Justice Committee is amazingly good with volunteers. I've honestly never seen such an organization so attentive — they care so much for their volunteers that you want to stay involved with them. I think it's a wonderful quality.

We now get far more applications for volunteers than we can accept. When we look through the applications we are more interested in the applicant's purpose and career objectives than in their experience. If volunteers are motivated to learn, we will do what we can to make their stay with us meaningful while giving them the tools and guidance they need to build their capacities. Our aim is for the interns and volunteers working with us to be empowered with relevant skills to the extent possible for their future careers.

Once we had changed our expectations for volunteers and put more structure around the volunteer program, we experienced greater reliability and consistency in the volunteers' involvement. The more these roles became defined, the more successful we were at attracting even more participation. The definition of volunteer roles is most evident in our internship programs. Specific positions are offered, with clear responsibilities and requirements, for applicants to consider. We have internships in journalism, magazine production and layout, magazine marketing and promotion, workshop animation, fundraising and event coordination. Interns complete a minimum of 150 hours of work, but most do more than that, and often extend their stay with us past the scheduled completion date. Volunteers contribute fewer hours and so take on less responsibility, but the focus of their work is similarly defined.

How Does the Office Run?

We usually have about fifty volunteers work with us, in volunteer teams, work groups and individually. For the most part, the volunteers crowd into our small office and work at one of a dozen computer stations. Not all at the same time, fortunately! Many are in for one day of the week, so the demand for office space is spread out. A few contribute from outside the office, although we like to have volunteers come in at least once in a while to ensure there is good communication flow and to ensure they get feedback and guidance. Others, like the theatre groups, get together wherever they can get space to

Our volunteers took to the streets when the president of the Inter-American Development Bank (IDB) came to Montreal for a speech. At the time, the IDB was not keeping up with the rest of the world in recognizing and cancelling Third World debt. Derek MacCuish photo

rehearse, whenever they can find time (midnight sessions aren't uncommon) and don't come in to the office at all.

We usually have a list of things we want to do to make our volunteer program more effective. There always seem to be improvements to make. These are some of the ways we've found so far that help:

- Organize the daily routine: The office environment and capacity is fixed — a dozen well-equipped computer workstations in an informal, comfortable, non-intimidating work environment. The coffee's on before volunteers arrive. They are asked not to show up before 10:00 a.m. so the Director can have a bit of quiet time for phone calls and emails and to get the coffee started.
- Set up a schedule for each volunteer: We ask the volunteers to commit to a schedule which they set up (as long as it provides for at least one half-day of work per week) and mark themselves in on our big schedule board. Lunch and coffee breaks are not scheduled. The first work assignments are usually pretty light, until we get a sense of the person's capacities and commitment to us, and then increase in responsibility.
- Ensure a relaxed atmosphere and a sense of community: There is no

dress code, and it's okay to work with music on (or with earphones). The volunteers come from all around the world, which creates a culturally diverse work atmosphere. We sometimes have a potluck meal together, where there is more opportunity for volunteers to get to know each other. This is also a good time for them to talk about their experience with us and share ideas.

- Provide a simple guide to office procedures: We are currently creating an office procedure guide which will include basic logistics such as phone numbers, email and telephone protocols, as well as how to use the office network and filing system in the network functions. This helps avoid little mishaps (which can turn into big headaches for us), such as having to remind each volunteer to stop saving all their work on the desktop of whichever computer they happened to be assigned and not to name file folders after themselves.

- Good communication is key: We check in frequently with each volunteer to see how things are going, if the work is appropriate and do our best to ensure that they are enjoying a positive and rewarding experience. Since we are located in Montreal, the language of communication is usually a mix of English and French and occasionally Spanish.

- Devote staff time for volunteer coordination: Volunteer coordination is challenging in terms of time management for our staff. The training and supervision takes time and energy; if these are shaky, there is a good chance the relationship will not work out and the volunteer will not continue. So there is a constant demand on the staff to allocate appropriate and rewarding work for the volunteers.

- Form small groups to work on specific activities: We form ad hoc volunteer working teams with particular shared objectives. One person is assigned responsibility to coordinate communication between team members and take the lead in communicating to the appropriate staff person who should also be clearly identified. The team approach works for us in large part because the volunteers are mainly of the same age, engaged in university studies and are highly sociable with shared interests. They eventually become friends.

Who Are Our Volunteers?

The SJC volunteers come, literally, from all over the world — mostly from one of the following groups:

- University students: Many of our volunteers are university students living and studying in the centre of Montreal. We are fortunate to be located within easy reach of a large number of university students. Our office is a few blocks from one English-language university, a twenty minute walk from the other. We also have interns from the two French-language universities, located further away but still within easy reach by public transit. The students usually stay with us for three or four months, the period matching their school term.

> Tine came from France to intern as part of her final academic requirements. She had contacted several Montreal-area NGOs as she completed studies in Aix-en-Provence, and we were one of the very few who replied and encouraged her. After she was with us a couple of weeks she asked if we were interested in putting on a little film festival on aspects of African economic development. All the staff were supportive, and she put together a series of films paired with discussion panels and guest speakers. Shown at different locales, including one evening that also featured African food, the films drew full audiences and inspired a lot of discussion of African social and financial hardships.

- People between jobs: Some volunteers are between jobs and wanting to do helpful and fulfilling work until a job comes through. Others are new arrivals to Canada, waiting for official status that will allow them to stay (but in the meantime, they are restricted from taking employment). As a fellow from Ireland said, "I'm just sitting in the apartment going crazy, and thought that I might as well come here and do something." Their time with us varies and depends on circumstances, but usually the job-seekers aren't with us long — employers show interest in the résumés of self-motivated people with a history of community involvement and volunteering.
- Retired people: Some of our volunteers are older — retired or semi-retired. Their interests and motivations are different from the students and they stay with us for much longer periods of time.

> Velda and Lorraine work as a team doing the banking and accounts, cashing and writing the cheques and tracking the income and spending. They are practical, common-sense women with a strong sense of ethical obligation — and a joy in fulfilling it. Steadfast, consistent, confident in laying it on the line for the Director, they have been invaluable.

In general, while the students respond best if they can identify specific accomplishments that they will attain in their time with us, the older volunteers see the value of contributing to the ongoing health and efficiency of the organization.

- Interns: The interns give much greater time commitments and are given higher levels of responsibility than other volunteers. They are usually with us for three or six months, working several days a week. They get to know about a broader range of programs, take on much more responsibility and get more opportunity to contribute ideas and suggestions. Interns who are especially motivated and capable take on projects from conception to realization. Interns have been responsible for many successful initiatives, including workshops, the theatre project and the volunteer blog. They usually work with their own teams of volunteers, taking control of projects under the supervision of a staff person. The Director and the staff usually assess the feasibility of the project first, and if it's a good idea, it's a go!

Over time we've refined the internships, which used to be largely undefined. We used to work with individual interns on a case-by-case basis to identify their capabilities and how they match our needs and from there create the internship responsibilities. Then we realized we were not getting internships in areas where we needed them so we created specific placements and asked for applications. At the same time, we began communicating with the internship offices at local universities and formalizing our processes — the internship description, the time frame, the hour requirements and the responsibilities of the three parties involved (our office, the intern and the school). Working with the internship programs at local universities (two English, two French) and other learning institutions, we've built a good reputation as a place where interns are treated well and get solid work experience.

As examples of our internship positions, we developed two internships specific to the publishing of our magazine, the *Upstream Journal*. First we had a journalism internship for writers, then one for layout and graphic design. More recently we created an internship for marketing and building readership. This position comes with a lot of responsibility because it involves the whole image and direction of the magazine — the kind of audience that the magazine has or wants, how the magazine should be shaped to attract a larger audience, what kind of content it should have and what kind of look we should give it — in other words what kind of personality it should have.

What Makes a Successful Volunteer Experience?

I'm a teacher in a college now and everything I know about teaching, I've learned through SJC. Everything I know about teaching in a way that makes students want to learn and be involved and be interactive, I've learned through my experience with this organization.

- Having a meaningful experience: These days, what we hear most when we talk with our volunteers about their experience here is that it is meaningful to them. They want to be engaged in social justice issues in ways that match their time and ability and resonates with their sense of morality while contributing to their professional development. They also want to see, and be proud of, the results of their efforts. That seems to be critical to how we function as a volunteer-based organization — the experience should be meaningful for all of the individuals who come to us and contribute their time and labour.

- Clarity of objectives: From our experience, we see that precision and clarity in volunteer direction is key to getting and keeping motivated people. For example, we can't just ask a volunteer for some background research on a situation. We have to show why we need it and how the information will be used in our programs: "We need some statistics for tomorrow's press release condemning the coup in Honduras," rather than "Can you see what you can find out about what's going on in Honduras?" The more we can identify objectives and give purpose to their work, the better. Sometimes this takes a bit of time, as we assess their abilities and interests and match these to where we need help. It is more important that there be active interest on the part of the volunteer that we can tap in to, even in the absence of experience and training in most cases.

- Providing opportunities to develop practical skills: We want to ensure that volunteers can develop practical skills and add substance to their resumes. We view volunteering with us as a learning and skill-building process and so we provide the guidance and instruction. We also have some training resources, such as our "Guidelines of Best Practice in Communications and Writing Skills." These include how to write for the *Upstream Journal* magazine and how to write a press release or an action alert bulletin. Our guide to effective campaigning has fifty pages of advocacy techniques. We also have books on subjects like communications and graphic design that we encourage volunteers to borrow.

Volunteers often say they are surprised when they reflect on what they've learned here and realize the skills they've gained. For us, it's mainly a matter of giving talented, motivated individuals an opportunity to perform.

What Do We Do When Things Don't Work Out?

Not every volunteer with us does well. Sometimes, we can slip up by misjudging a person's interests and capabilities or because of demands on our time and energy, and so we do occasionally get a person who has problems with things like incomplete work, missed deadlines or lack of follow through on commitments.

It's not unusual for volunteers to be self-interested to a degree. The volunteer applications we receive usually describe their interest in the area in which we work — Third World poverty and human rights — and express their desire to contribute to improving the world. Many describe how they want to develop skills that will help their career develop. Very few mention

Our theatre program is different every year, depending on which way our volunteers want to take it, but it's always interactive and fun political theatre. Since 1996 the troupe has brought its satire to a variety of settings, including restaurants, city parks, high schools and downtown theatres. Mar Armstrong photo

any benefit to the organization but we know that we are included when they generalize about wanting to help make a difference in some way.

Problems can arise if their motivations don't really include us once they are here. We have an accountability process in place. The volunteers and interns are accountable to one of the two staff supervisors who are in turn accountable to the Board of Directors. Supervisors are responsible for guiding the volunteers and ensuring their stay with us is productive and fulfilling. If it is not, they are responsible to correct it and this includes those rare times when the relationship isn't working and should end.

Once in a while, a volunteer is unable to get beyond self-involvement and realize that sharing our objectives and ambitions is also a critical part of their time with us. They show up occasionally and do some quick tasks that may or may not be adequate. They don't get assigned responsibilities of any significance, don't become part of a project or team, don't form friendships as the others do and fade away, often without a goodbye.

The last time we went through a hiring process, we asked applicants how they would deal with a volunteer that wasn't working out. Almost without exception, the applicants said they'd take the person aside and try to see if there were issues that needed attention. Perhaps there were personal dynamics and built-up stress that needed sorting out in order to make things work. It's all well-intentioned, but we explain to them that our preference is to make our expectations as clear as possible, taking into account abilities and time constraints. People who have repeated trouble with time management or in balancing other demands and responsibilities should deal with it themselves. If problems with their work are chronic, we don't spend too much time looking for solutions. We move on, as do they. Fortunately, these situations are rare.

They Want to Change the World, We Want to Help Them Do It

Our organization depends on the volunteers, although we do get donations from many individuals and communities that see the value of our work. Funding for the work we do is very limited. Therefore, we train our volunteers and trust them with responsibility; in turn, they come back, again and again, to accept that responsibility and take on the work with eagerness and pleasure. To end our chapter, here's a success story from a volunteer:

> After Hurricane Mitch hit Nicaragua and Honduras, we went on quite a strong campaign to convince the Canadian Government to cancel the debts owed to Canada from those countries, saying: "This is inhumane. It was already terrible that you were collecting those debts in the first place, but now these countries have faced such devastation, its simply unacceptable that you should continue to collect those debts"… Canada did cancel the debts… [the campaign] was a major success.

Note

1.   All quotes are from staff or volunteers interviewed about their involvement with the Social Justice Committee.

10

STORYTELLERS' FOUNDATION

LEARNING FOR A CHANGE

Anne Docherty

Behold the miracle of the accordion.
It's an instrument that shouldn't work but it does.
Accordions are so improbable they should be considered in the same scrap heap of
unlikely miracles as unexpected apologies and grassroots movements.

Speaking to you, you who take on difficult things.

You wake up on most days to your duty and tend to the delicate gardens of human
needs in spite of the nagging certainty that any minute now it might all get paved.

You strap yourselves to the PA system even when it's difficult to prove that anyone
is listening. Ideas that used to be played often and openly are now holding the dust
up in slumbering attics.

How are you supposed to get anything done when general interest in the way the
world is going has become an instrument too shameful to play in public?

Consider the accordion.

Frankly, when you start cataloguing what can go wrong on an instrument where
everything can go wrong then the moments where everything is okay become sublime.

The accordion is not an ideal machine like a Swiss watch or an academic essay,
the parts do not mesh perfect but in this everyday fragility I see a kind of gallantry.
Pick your favourite thing in the world. A sunset, chocolate, the community where
you perform your labours.

If you look closely enough everything that we love is like this — difficult, pitted by
accident and full of things that break. But this is the measure of our luck, to be here

together and to be willing to wear the responsibility of loving the unlikely.

We shouldn't be able to do this and yet our readiness creates a particular beauty that can be considered in the same stubborn category as a donkey kick, kitchen sink politics and the resolution to keep moving. Failure becomes too familiar to deserve a name.

Here we are. Listen to the rattles. Listen to the unpleasant sounds you can make; the obstinate opposite of harps and angels, the confusion of too many hearts having to find a way.

We are the poster children of the especially unlikely miracle.
And yet behold we still work. (Adler 2009)

Important Challenges

The Accordion is a spoken word poem by Barbara Adler. We invited Barbara to attend our annual symposium and perform a poem as a wrap up activity. The symposium used music (accordions and cello) and art as well as conversation as vehicles for community educators and organizers to reflect on their work and ask honest questions of each other. This annual symposium creates a space away from the busyness of "doing" to spend time thinking and learning. For us, it's important to remember that learning (an activity designed for the purpose of understanding the world around us) is what creates change. And that learning is only fully realized with reflection on our actions.

At our most recent symposium we posed two guiding questions that reflect the tensions existing among organizations who hold a social justice frame in our region: "How do we organize ourselves economically so that we can sustain the work of organizing and learning at the grassroots level?" and, "Are we remaining focused on social change work or have we fallen in to social service delivery?

About Us

People often call our organization inquiring about storytelling workshops. That's not exactly what we do. The name Storytellers' Foundation was created because we want to support people to tell their own story. Our name reminds us that this is our work — to find ways to support individuals and groups to build the skills, knowledge or confidence necessary to assert their rights and responsibilities as a citizen. Our name was created when one of our founding staff members was on a journalism fellowship to the Poynter Institute in Florida. His interest was on how to use media to engage a disengaged population. He wanted to develop the concept of a magazine that reflected First Nations people in its pages and discussed issues that were relevant to an Indigenous readership. The name Storytellers' Foundation was born. Although the original idea was to use media to engage people, we have kept the name and now use many forms of community organizing to engage an active citizenry.

Storytellers' Foundation started after the first set of Treaty talks (Gitxsan, British Columbia and Canada) ended in the mid-1990s. A few of us had been involved in public education about the treaty and, although we were told that people find it hard to work together, we were witnessing people willing to talk with each other, overcome differences of opinion so they could live together as neighbours and have the courage to learn about and talk about sensitive issues. This inspired us. We left that work feeling energized and excited to belong to our community and we were especially interested in how learning together was leading to action together. The Gitxsan chiefs who had led this treaty process told us they wanted the work of engaging people (especially young people) to continue. They liked how Gitxsan and non-Gitxsan were imagining a culturally diverse community where people worked together to increase both social and economic assets while sustaining healthy ecosystems. And so we rented a building in Hazelton, BC and evolved in to our present structure, which is a non-profit society with a Board of Directors that directs and supports us and a staff to carry out project activities. Storytellers' staff and board are both Gitxsan and non-Gitxsan. All staff members live in the community. Staff hold formal education in community economic development, informal education, community organizing and international development. The majority of staff have lived most of their lives in this area.

Storytellers' Foundation has always had an interest in the political aspect of learning — especially informal learning — that happens daily in the community. We believe that learning creates change. We are interested in learning more about how community groups organize opportunities for learning in order to foster democratic participation. We are especially interested in highlighting how the act of learning, when facilitated in the community, heightens citizen development and increases engagement.

Our vision is that of an active citizenship who involves itself in value-based and democratic decision making. Our main vehicle to realize that vision is our storefront, known as the "Learning Shop." Within the Learning Shop we have five focus areas: Community Development Learning and Literacy, Research and Development, Peer Learning, Local Food Systems and Solidarity Cooperatives.

It's important for us to know our values and to share our values with everyone we work with. In turn we create time and an environment for others to share their values with us. Our values include:

- Social Justice: enabling people to claim their human rights and have greater control over decision-making processes which affect their lives.
- Ecology: resisting the homogenization of people and their practices and slowing down climate change through our daily practice, information and knowledge sharing.
- Learning: recognizing the skills, knowledge, confidence and attitudes that we each hold and need to develop to tackle social, economic, political and environmental issues.
- Cooperation: working together to identify and implement social, political, economic and environmental action.
- Participation: facilitating democratic involvement by people in the issues that affect their lives based on autonomy, shared power, skills, knowledge and experience.
- Equality: challenging attitudes and practices that discriminate against and marginalize people.

Living in Relationship

A couple of years ago, on leaving the office we see Old Neil, Big Ward and Bill drive by. That day it looked like they'd been berry picking, but they could have been mushrooming or checking the trap line. Old Neil is now 97 years old. He is a *sim'oogyet*. Recently, at a feast for our service-learning program, he explained the meaning of *sim'oogyet* to the group. "Write this down," he said, "then you'll know what I've said and then you'll know the meaning of *sim'oogyet*. Walk by people and look them in the eye and say hello, be friendly and be caring because now you know the meaning of *sim'oogyet*."

Big Ward was 99 years old when he died last year. His eyesight had started to fail so he had stopped trapping. He was famous for his pancake breakfasts on Sunday morning for anyone who stopped by — and many did. We used to enjoy his stories of how he'd argue with his daughter that Gordon Campbell is a gentleman who should be listened to because the Bible tells us to follow our leaders. His daughter, Alice Maitland, 77 years old, would get mad and strongly disagree. Alice is our mayor of thirty years. "Prickly like a porcupine," is how Big Ward lovingly described his daughter — "fighting with me since she entered this world."

Bill, who drove with these two on a regular basis, is 78 years old and Alice's husband. They are what we call "land-based citizens," people deeply connected to place. Relationships that have been woven for one hundred years and relationships that have been woven for 10,000 years shape their families. Knowledge of living on this land and with this land has been passed on from generation to generation. Because of these relationships they can disagree and still live with care for one another. Because of this knowledge they can live a sustenance lifestyle that keeps them healthy and engaged, regardless of cyclical global economies. They see themselves as part of the ecosystem they live with, not apart from it. This knowledge and these relationships are the foundation of community learning.

That same day as we left the office we see one of our "kids" passed out on the street. We walked over to make sure he was still breathing and hadn't choked on his own vomit. As we were checking on him, his girlfriend walked by. "Get up," she yelled, "or I'll get hold of your granny and you'll be in real trouble." He swore at her but did, miserably, crawl on to his hands and feet. He then staggered up the hill before his granny found out he was lying drunk in the middle of the road. Somehow in the depth of his despair and lack of esteem he still felt enough connection to not want his granny to be mad at him or to be shamed. We wonder if it is because of local knowledge that he still had enough connection and sense of belonging to get up and go home. If he lived elsewhere, would he care or be able to act on the threat of his granny finding out?

Our recent social and economic history has damaged but not severed these relationships to kin and to land. Our current social and economic climate continues to threaten the passing on of local knowledge. The history and current course of colonization and corporatism continues to influence the contradictions we see in our community.

Success to us means that people living here recognize, and act on, the knowledge they hold. Success involves more of us having the confidence and connection to see ourselves as part of "the glue" that holds community together. Success involves our public institutions of government, education, health and justice recognizing and validating remote, rural living and creating policies and practices that reflect ecologically-based frameworks. Success requires that we build allies beyond our own locality and connect with movements of change for social justice at home and beyond.

Learning in Community

One of our community development projects is the Good Food Box project. Even though it is called a "Good Food" project, we recognize that there is a lot that isn't "good" about it. The Good Food Box is available for a cost of $20 each month to anyone in the community. It is full of fruits and vegetables. We got tired of seeing fruits and vegetables being trucked in from thousands of kilometres away and still being so cheap because somewhere growers weren't getting paid a fair wage for their labour. So we decided to grow our food locally. We planted over five hundred pounds of potatoes, carrots, onions, beans, peas, zucchinis, squash and cabbage. When it came to harvest the hundreds of pounds of vegetables, we really needed help and so enlisted the volunteer efforts of high school students who were not finding success in school. They showed up one day not at all excited at the thought of pulling vegetables out of a dry, dusty field. We recognized the frustrations they held with teachers, with the job they'd been handed that day and at life in general, but persuaded them to give us a hand anyway. As we led them down the path to the field one boy noticed the raspberries and another the cranberries. He yelled and took off to pick and eat, his friends laughed at him but slowly joined him and, as they found big, juicy berries, their attitudes started to change. One boy mentioned he was starving and hadn't eaten anything all morning, the others joined in with their stories of hunger. We moved on to the field and yelled back for them to see what we had found; they started eating peas and pulling carrots, dusting them off and taking huge bites in between grins and laughter. They forgot to be frustrated with the world, they forgot to be sluggish teenagers, they just became boys who hadn't been fed that day and hadn't felt listened to in a long time. They told us stories about their lives, their teachers told them stories about when they had been kids. We were simply local people enjoying the company of each other.

When we learn in community we are learning as neighbours. We are learning with and from each other. We are learning to articulate the values and visions we hold. We are learning to take action together so that the changes we want will happen. When we, as land-based citizens, have the opportunity to design the learning framework, it is our local knowledge that frames the learning process. Our natural ways of relating and our natural practices on the land inform us of what is necessary to know.

When we learn in community we learn in order to find meaning in the world around us. We learn in relationship and we learn for change. We have the comfort of knowing that the learning relationships are life-long because, as rural and land-based people, we aren't leaving home any time soon. This lets us be intentional and it lets us be organic. We have time to evolve and nurture relationships. We have time for the learning process of animation (wake up), formation (develop skills and knowledge) and finally education (to lead or take charge). Knowing this gives us hope. And, knowing the loving relationships that exist all around us sustains our hope. Our kids are struggling and our elders are still here. Our job as community educators is to facilitate the relationships. That is where and how learning takes place in our community.

Organizing for Change

We recently attended a book launch. The book was titled, *Good Intentions Gone Awry*. That title spoke volumes to us. Our "kids" are struggling because of good intentions that are often misguided and damaging. Our Canadian public institutions have create conceptual frameworks that are based on an epistemology that is counterproductive to the beliefs, practices and ways of holding and transferring knowledge in our community.

We want to change the dependency that has resulted from our recent social and economic history. We want to foster interdependence so that young people in our communities are actively involved in decision-making that reflect the values and visions that our community has so clearly articulated. We want our young people to learn how to do things that reflect local values and visions, and we want our public institutions to be flexible enough for this to happen.

Conditions that Foster Success

It's great to be involved with youth and kids at the Learning Shop, planting seeds and showing them how to plant. It's great because very few learn it at home on a parent-to-child basis. And learning to grow food becomes a catalyst in a community because people who grow food for themselves, well there's a camaraderie — a reason to get together and talk and know we are together in this with the common denominator being the earth in which our seeds are planted.

As human beings we are born into social relationships and we live in relationship with others for the rest of our lives. Our sense of self and a sense of community is formed through interaction with others. Through our conversations and our reciprocal exchanges we develop relationships with others. These relationships in turn help us create a sense of attachment, a sense of belonging and a sense of communion with others. Like dropping a pebble into a pond, there is a rippling affect that broadens out the sense of community and our participation in it, person by person, interaction by interaction, relationship by relationship. These direct and informal relationships create a level of trust that is essential to creating the norms of reciprocity and building the social networks that lead to acts of collaboration. Trust and reciprocity are the pillars of any sound partnership. These qualities enable us to take risks and deal with the uncertainty that is inherent in community development efforts.

Robert Putnam (2000: 19) uses the term "social capital" to refer to

> connections among individuals — social networks and the norms of reciprocity and trustworthiness that arise from them. In this sense social capital is closely related to what some have called "civic virtue." The difference is that "social capital" calls attention to the fact that civic virtue is most powerful when embedded in a network of reciprocal social relations. A society of many virtuous but isolated individuals is not necessarily rich in social capital.

James Coleman (1988), in turn, talks about the importance of social capital to the development of human capital. Coleman argues that a person's ability to develop skills and capacities (human capital) that make them able to act in new ways is supported where trust is exercised by the mutual acceptance of obligations, where there is an open exchange of ideas and information and where norms and sanctions encourage people to work for a common good. It is the interaction between human and social capital that creates the dynamic for the emergence of a learning community.

Although we have years of professional training and experience in informal education and community development, we are not simply workers in a project. We are community members who have developed relationships and personal connections to people within the community on many different levels. We are "in community." We are part of the dynamic process of creating community and social change with others.

We believe that finding ways to enhance the quality of these relationships and networks is at the core of work "in community." The fundamental purpose of such work is to create the conditions that let reciprocity, honesty, trust, ideas, shared action and a sense of communion emerge from the community so that, in the words of John Dewey, "people can build a shared life together" (Dewey and Archambault 1964). We believe that the quality of life in the community is dependent upon the quality and nature of our relationships with others. And in our community, despite the social and economic ills, our relationships are profound and caring and animated with reciprocity.

Making Hope Concrete

A group of young adults who had not found success with formal learning were supported to explore the question, "What does it take to get back in the door of learning?" One young woman on the team suggested we take it back even further: "Forget getting in the door of learning! What does it take to get out of bed in the morning?" They created a poster as a the result of their exploration. It describes capacities that young adults in Hazelton recognize they need to take control of their lives (personal power) and to organize for change in the community (political power). The team talked with people who had been influences in their lives and identified seven learning environments where personal and political power is fostered. As they talked to other youth and described how they had developed each element, the team recognized that they were also capable of influencing others. They recognized that as they were learning they were also teaching. The poster reminds us that we all play important roles as teachers in the community in fostering and nurturing personal and political power.

The role of Storytellers' Foundation is to make explicit the learning that takes place in the informal arenas of community. These places are often overlooked. It is within these informal arenas that people are becoming educated. And yet, many are not even aware that they are learning or educating themselves. What we try to do is make learning explicit. We want to validate the informal learning that takes place daily in our lives. We want to heighten our intent in educating citizens. It is in the informal learning arenas that social change occurs. People start recognizing they hold power. People start naming what's important to them and articulating what they want.

This approach of recognizing and fostering informal learning arenas creates opportunity for people to learn what they need, when they need it, in a way that serves their level of understanding. It puts a process in place, locally, to ensure that those who aren't engaging in public life have support to do so. It is a system that nurtures and promotes citizen curiosity, reflection and informed action. It requires local control where decisions start at home and are then supported by more removed decision makers. It demands flexible and open systems for learning. And it results in people learning together and taking action together.

It is these places where informal learning takes place that Barbara Adler speaks about in her poem:

> Here we are. Listen to the rattles. Listen to the unpleasant sounds you can make; the obstinate opposite of harps and angels, the confusion of too many hearts having to find a way.
>
> We are the poster children of the especially unlikely miracle.
> And yet behold we still work.

11

ACTIVISM THAT WORKS

EMERGENT THEMES

Avery Calhoun, Maureen Wilson and Elizabeth Whitmore

> Storytelling reveals meaning without committing the error of defining it. (Hannah Arendt)

The stories from activist authors provide perspectives on meanings and facilitators of success from as deep an insider perspective as possible — the position of people participating in the day-to-day efforts of the groups or organizations. Other dimensions emerge when meanings and facilitators of success are considered from an inter-partner — or broad-spectrum — perspective. Our interviews with eighty-six activists are the basis on which, in this chapter, we provide responses to the question, "What did the activists convey to us about the range of meanings to them of success or effectiveness in their work, and about factors that facilitate success?" Not surprisingly, there is considerable overlap between the two. Steps along the way to broader goals may be in the moment experienced as successes in themselves and — vice versa — achievements may be retrospectively identified as steps along the way to different outcomes.

In this chapter we summarize the themes that emerged from what activists told us about meanings of success and what facilitates it. It is impossible to convey the affect that accompanied the words we are reporting here — the energy, excitement and deep commitment communicated in our encounters with these remarkable people. For us, it was almost invariably uplifting. As much as possible, we have the activists speak for themselves in relation to these themes.

What Does Success Mean to Social Activists?

For the activists, success or effectiveness in their work has a number of intersecting meanings. While sharing a desire for transformational change

— for broad social, political, economic and environmental justice — the groups described to us a rich range of indicators that tell them when their own work is successful. These include concrete changes in policies, practices or laws; citizen engagement; aspects of the functioning of the activist groups themselves; raising awareness or changing attitudes of politicians, decision-makers and the general public; and personal change for activist group members themselves.

Broad Social/Environmental Justice Goals
Activists from all groups in this project identified broad transformative goals: "Well you know success comes when people who are poor and oppressed are no longer poor and oppressed." People told us of envisioning a time when "the world is at peace and we have a handle on all of the environmental problems." Some described "the total elimination of racism, the total elimination of sexism and homophobia" and others, "no poverty in the world for children. All children are going to school. No child is dying of HIV/AIDS."

Changes in Policies, Practices or Laws
While keeping broader goals of social transformation always in mind, people told us they assess success in terms of specific "concrete" outcomes — changes in policies, practices or laws in their own spheres of activity. For example, "Canada did cancel the debts... Yeah, it was a major success" or

> Finally we got [the accelerated capital cost allowance] removed from the federal budget in 2007. And by doing so, we put back in the pockets of Canadians... hundreds of millions of dollars in revenue.

Success was celebrated when laws were enacted: "to have inclusion of sexual orientation [in the Individual Rights Protection Act]" and policies changed: "McMaster and Guelph adopted a fair trade policy." For Alberta's social workers, achieving mandatory registration meant that the ethical obligation of their profession to pursue social justice was now enshrined in legislation:

> Being included in the Health Professions Act] has given a voice to our clients that they didn't have without it... The fact that six thousand social workers are under the legislation... and are accountable to the public we serve.

Sometimes, activist groups told us, they were fortunate enough to be able not only to influence changes in policy or regulations, but also to observe the human and/or environmental impacts of these changes: "The campaign was to get them kicking in more money in aid for education. And so it was very, very successful in making things happen. Lots of kids went to school as a result."

Even where not successful in terms of the explicit, identified objective, there were sometimes still identifiable gains:

> What we were trying to achieve was a twenty percent increase in welfare rates. It wasn't successful, but from the point of view of raising the profile of social workers, I think it was very successful.

Participants frequently identified pitfalls related to characterizing only these observable or measurable types of outcomes as successes. Achieving change may mean "a long, slow process," of which they may never see the full results. Further, the concern was expressed that too much reliance on "measureable" outcomes might "force people to choose, as advocacy targets, quantifiable things that aren't necessarily systemic change."

Many advocacy groups acknowledged the impossibility of knowing whether any given event or action actually "causes" a result.[1] Inevitably, many forces, conditions and players are involved and it is thus difficult to credit a successful outcome to any one cause.

> When we define success… it is changing government policy. Changing bad policy into good policy. Now the problem with that is there's always an attribution question, so we can play a role in that, but there are so many other roles… You could have a really progressive Prime Minister, you could have huge public concern, and again, environmental groups can play a role in that, but they're only [a] part…. You could have a spate of news media stories… a huge number of factors that go into a political decision.

Citizen Engagement

Democratic participation or citizen engagement is widely identified by activists as an end in itself.[2] The level of success of this engagement is seen as evidenced in the numbers of people participating, in who those participants are, and in the nature or quality of that participation. The numbers of people engaged was identified as an important outcome especially in relation to public gatherings such as rallies or demonstrations and, of course, for signatures on petitions. Regarding who is engaged, the diversity of people engaged in social justice activities is also widely valued: "There will be First Nation kids, white kids, older people, all together. To me, I think that's just the most amazing part." Many groups see it as important that people engaging in social action are not just "the usual suspects," the ubiquitous, hard core activists: "Marching down that street, that feeling in Calgary, with such a wide range of middle class people and people with children… soccer mums. It was wonderful." And, "You begin to see those [ideas taken up by]… people who are calling in to talk shows or people who are being interviewed on the street for the news."

Sometimes even more than the numbers or identities of the people engaged, the nature or quality of people's engagement is celebrated. People told us they value risk-taking, nonviolence, civility, collaboration, self-advocacy and, to some most importantly, just the fact that people are standing up and making themselves heard.

We noticed that significant energy and excitement among group members at opposite ends of the age spectrum as they told stories about "breaking the rules." For the Raging Grannies, this animation comes through in their description of the experience of crashing then Prime Minister Paul Martin's Stampede breakfast. As they were escorted out by security, "[We had] a long line of Liberals to sing to. I mean you adapted to the immediate circumstances… And it wasn't really singing to Paul Martin; it was singing to his constituents." When the same group had its request turned down to present at city hall to a committee meeting on pesticide use:

> What we were going to do to make our representation was to sing our dandelion songs and present the members of this committee with dandelions… [they] asked us to leave… We went out singing: "Without the right to protest, where would we be? There would be no votes for women yet, and no democracy."

Many activists spoke with satisfaction of the nonviolent nature of their work, especially where there may have been fears that it could be otherwise:

> So yeah, [the police] infiltrated us… but maybe that was good, because they learned that we didn't want violence. The bulk of all these organizers, we didn't want that. And we were working really hard not to get that.

Engaging people of opposing views in civil public dialogue was considered a particular success by some of activists.

> A Canadian mine company is trying to build a gold mine in San Marco in Guatemala. We opposed it because the company has not consulted the local community. But the way we do it, we held a conference between four parties: the guy from the World Bank (this project is financed by the World Bank)… and then a representative from Friends of Earth and then the representative from the mining company and also the Archbishop from that community in San Marcos. So four of them came together and then they had a conference… And to me, something like that is especially good, because it brings people together, and people from different perspectives. Even though they don't agree with each other, but this is a place where they can exchange ideas, you know. And trying to understand better… Just the fact that we could bring people together to talk about the issue, to me, it's a success. Because, sure, issues like that cannot be solved just by having a conference or anything… At the end of the conference, no agreement has reached, right? The company hasn't agreed, "Okay, yeah, you're right. We should stop doing that." It is not that easy and life is complex, but at least the people are together, they talk about it and we make people think about it.

For the Disability Action Hall, making one's voice heard can be seen as an important success in itself. Advocating for one's own and others' rights, publicly voicing one's opinion, is highly valued:

> I feel proud when we do the rallies, our speak-out rallies. Our Louder and Prouder Rallies every year. Because we're able to come out and show, "Yes, we have a disability and we're not shy to show that we have one, that we can be loud, like loud and proud about it."

This includes children and youth:

> It was having kids' participation, kids at risk. They were kids out of the prison systems… and we were able to have young people put questions to the MPs, thoughtful questions. And questions that clearly reflected their falling through the system. You know kids who… came there out of detention programs.

and engaging with issues internationally:

> In the "For All" campaign on public services, we were promoting access to public services… You know we have a group of students in St. John who are willing to go on the street corner and sit on toilets on World Toilet Day, to talk about the importance of sanitation and get a pretty interesting picture on the front page of the paper.

The presence of energy and enthusiasm was widely identified as an important sign that things are going well: "People investing their energy is always a measure or a sign of success. And people just being enthusiastic." And, "When we were at the activity… the atmosphere, the enthusiasm, the pride, just the participation was overwhelming… Everybody there was smiling, everybody was happy."

Changing Attitudes or Atmosphere Around an Issue

While shifting attitudes or atmosphere around an issue may be seen as mainly a means to an end, for specific pieces of work this in itself is seen as a sign of the success of their efforts.

> There are two objectives we have. We set a particular policy objective. You know we say… this is what we want to change. And so, you measure success as to whether you change it or not… Another major level… is the building of awareness and reaffirming of attitudes and beliefs broadly in society. And that's a long-term one that happens through a lot of different activities we undertake. But the campaign has to help move that along and that's much more difficult to measure. But it's crucial, particularly over the long-term.

Many of the activists believe that changes in awareness or attitudes can produce changes in behaviour and thus a major difference in quality of life for some people: "The more people we have in the school who don't tolerate homophobia, which will translate into other intolerant language and behaviour in the school… the better that makes the schools and society."

For members of the Disability Action Hall, reframing the meaning of disability was described as having hugely empowering implications for both their self-esteem and for their approach to activism.

> I really appreciate those opportunities where you make someone question. They ask… "Why are you… celebrating disability?" "Why are you calling it Freak Out?" Like, "That's so wrong, you shouldn't be proud." And then someone with disability goes, "But I am and what's wrong with that?" [A certain Hall member] has been confronted a few times by people who are TABS (temporarily able bodied, he calls them). And he just… challenges people.

Others emphasize the importance of their roles in framing and informing public policy debates:

> The fact that there was a public review process for us was a victory in that we had been calling for that to happen. And there were certainly certain elements of how the Panel undertook its work that reflected our recommendations.

> It's the highest compliment when your information is good enough that you convince one of your key audiences who can influence other audiences to carry your message. So when you start to see your messages as newspaper editorials that you had nothing to do with directly, you know you've gotten somewhere. That's when I knew we had made many breakthroughs on that issue. We started to see writers, we started to see other politicians, we started to see people talking about this issue in terms that we had framed it.

and in influencing government thinking:

> We did do the submission to the Senate Committee Report and got the Senate Committee Report to quote us. I mean that's one measure of success. You got that right; they're using it. How many times are you quoted in the report to which you made a submission? And we're well-quoted.

Raising awareness among specific target groups was identified as an aim of all of the groups. Politicians (or their constituents) and decision-makers, for example, are frequently singled out for attention: "We visited targeted MPs across the country and we made sure to get to MPs of all different stripes. And ask that they take this campaign to the respective caucuses."

Attracting media coverage is often mentioned as evidence of success: "We could see every night on the news… if we were successful, if we got media attention and our particular voice was heard. And it quite often was." One participant commented on connections among various layers of media:

> An example of success is] launching a report that gets (a) good positive media cover-

age and (b) that even generates some debate and that appears as blogs on major media websites, for example. And (c) gets quoted by very reputable, well-known Canadian organizations in their own policy materials or at their events or when they're speaking to the media.

Media attention in itself is valued as a way of reaching people with a message. Fair, in-depth media coverage is considered even better: "I think that [our organization was] able to help the media better understand and report on some of the complex implications of some of this. And put an analysis out that was more balanced and fair."

Bringing awareness to the general public constitutes success in the view of many activists.

> Fifteen years ago, if you were to ask someone, "What is a sweat shop?" [the answer would have been] "I don't know." Whereas now, if you ask people "What is a sweat shop?" there is a fairly good idea about what a sweat shop is.

A member of the Pembina Institute talked about a campaign to raise awareness regarding the Alberta oil royalties regime:

> We identified over three years ago or so that the royalty system in Alberta was just not in the best interest… for the long-term success of Alberta. And so, we started raising awareness about that issue by publishing different papers on it, meeting with different influential people over time to raise their awareness about it. Writing opinion editorials in newspapers on it, getting some media coverage on it. And then, ensuring that it was brought up in our conversations with the different leadership candidates for the provincial PC Party. And then, that sort of became really mainstream.

Group Functioning

Many participants referred to the importance of aspects of the functioning of their groups. Internally, participants talked about teamwork as one vital aspect of what made their organizations effective. Building networks and collaboration among organizations was seen as essential to what effectiveness means, as was building a sense of community, attracting and retaining group members and the credibility or reputation of the group.

> There's an energy that's in the [activity], and I think that's what we've done best, is we've somehow articulated what that energy is. And all that energy is animating what we see when our community works best.

Continuity of participation among group members was regarded as a clear sign of success:

> One of the things that I see as being a success is that youth continually come back. And we have youth who come and come and come. And sometimes I'm like why are they here? But… there is a reason why they keep coming back. There are some

> who have been here forever, and there are only so many new things we can do. But here they are.

as was attracting the fresh energy of new people.

Personal Experience, Meaning, Learning

The struggle for social justice can be difficult and discouraging work. Change can be slow — at times, barely perceptible. Sometimes activists have a feeling of "tilting at windmills, because we're trying to take on big issues." People had interesting things to tell us about what keeps them going, what animates them, in their activist work. For many, it was a feeling of "being part of something that's bigger than yourself," "[when] you can see sort of a global movement, people taking action and that you're a part of that." Their commitment to making positive change in the world, along with a sense that they are joined in this by others, is a powerful combination:

> The passion of people involved — either volunteers or staff or participants — it's really about the cause and that is it. You know, it's not about anything else. So when people together, when they talk about stuff, there is always this energy in this environment. Like people are together doing something.

Feeling a part of something bigger — having "people who share the same vision and to have… a mutual commitment toward that vision" — gives hope of achieving change that could not be created by an individual alone:

> We realize that together we can make a difference. I know it sounds somewhat trite, but the fact is that we actually believe we can do it and we succeed. And I think that that's the key to it.

People told us they are further heartened in their desire to "do the right thing" when a "concrete" objective has been met, when they "hear the stories of people's lives being improved and the part the [organization] has played in that; it's extremely rewarding and worthwhile." "There is a good feeling when you help make something happen, like a Starbucks recognizing Ethiopia's rights to their own brand names for coffee." Others speak of a sense of belonging. One participant summed up what many felt about his organization: "One of the things this place offers… is a sense of community."

Constructing the space within which others feel empowered, to feel they can make a difference, is a high moment for some. "It's a wonderful moment… to get a chance to watch people kind of blossom." A staff member of the Disability Action Hall described a commitment to bringing together people of similar experience:

> To create action and a shared culture and a shared voice. And that's critical for people to change their lives. It's not going to happen one by one, [with] a disabled person

> connected to a non-disabled person. It's going to happen [with] a disabled person in a safe space, creating a voice with other disabled people.

For a disabled member of the same group, the meaning of success meant being in that shared space:

> A group of us from the Hall traveled to Edmonton to attend the self-advocacy summit and it was a conference over a weekend… I had never been in a gathering of self-advocates of that size before. Never had quite the same opportunity to talk to and share experiences with peers such as that before.

For groups in which membership is based on personal identification with the cause they are working on, success is to some extent defined by feelings of acceptance and validation of identity.

> I think it was successful for me because through the course of being together, sharing stories, talking about issues, talking about systemic barriers… we came to realize a lot of what we share and also, the gathering was not just about the discussion of problems, but it very much had the feel of a great big celebration of who we are as people and as disabled people. And through the celebration of this big collection, this big group of people, the celebration of who we are, I think we all left feeling a tremendous surge of pride in who we are and in what we do.

Sometimes that personal validation and acceptance morphs into a politicized involvement in the fight for social justice, in a shift of focus from the personal to the political:

> The Youth Project slowly built me up as a stronger individual, of being a LGBT youth and all of a sudden, the following year, I became… this big youth advocate for gay and lesbian students in my school. And everyone came to me for questions and came to me for support and yeah, I definitely think that if it wasn't for the Youth Project, I would have probably committed suicide… I know a lot of other youth who rely on this place a lot to get through even a week of their life.

The importance of having fun, feeling enthused and feeling cared for was widely mentioned. In an echo of Emma Goldman's "If I can't dance, I don't want to be part of your revolution,"[3] one youth observed that

> There's a lot of laughter, there's a lot of fun involved… So the process itself is kind of as rewarding, I find, as the result. And just the experience is very uplifting and positive and enjoyable. And that's definitely one of the motivators of being here… it's very enjoyable and its work, it's important work, but it's also fun.

Participants from several groups spoke passionately about what they had learned in the course of their activism — about the issues with which they are engaged and about themselves:

> I don't know if I can even explain half the things that I've learned from this work and that have developed me as a person. Which gives back to the community, which may change other people. That's a big thing, I think, in all the people that have worked here.

What Do Activists Believe Facilitates Success in Their Work?
Analysis of the Context to Find Opportunities for Action

Throughout our various interactions with these activists, we have been struck by how clearly they identified the importance of their ability to identify, analyze and act strategically in relation to conditions in their environments.

Conversations about relationships between broader social structures, local contexts and individual experience were among the most passionate, perhaps because the commitment to social justice derives in large part from their recognition of the structural causes of social inequities. Many participants were of the opinion that the world could really change if only all of us understood that "everything is connected." A Disability Action Hall staff member described the following:

> One meeting in particular, where we went around the group… and said: "Who's been to the food bank?" every disabled person there had been to the food bank in the last year. Not one ally had been to the food bank in the last year. "Who owns a car?" Not one disabled person had a car. Every ally had a car. "Who has been on a holiday in the last year?" Maybe one or two disabled people had been on little holidays. All of the allies had been on a holiday and nobody else had been. So we purposely would point this out. "Is it fair that all the non-disabled people in the room don't go to food bank, have a car, go on holidays, have a house, you know all those kinds of things and none of you do? Is that fair?" I mean we would just put that out really plainly… Not to make people feel bad, but partly to make people feel angry. "Is this fair? We don't think it's fair, do you think it's fair?"… I remember particularly a few weeks of just those really intense discussions, where people started to think differently about, "Maybe it's not fair that I have to go to the food bank."

Because structural analysis — understanding the broad social forces (and principal opposing interests) determining social structures — is considered foundational to achieving social justice goals, many groups develop strategies designed to help themselves and their constituencies (policy makers, politicians, their own members, the general public) to understand these connections. Some identify this process as "consciousness raising" or "connecting the personal and political." In one participant's words, "People start to become more conscious of their life experience and that maybe the issues they were experiencing weren't their fault, but they were political, structural issues." A person who was a stakeholder in one of the participating advocacy organizations described how well that organization made these connections:

> They deal with social implications, they deal with economic implications, they deal with ecological implications and they're very good at getting people to understand that all of these things are integrated. That, I think, is the fundamental biggest problem we have facing us in the future at the political level. Is that we've divided these three elements up in our minds and we've not been able to integrate. We tend to focus on one element only and forget about the rest. What Pembina is able to do… is to get people to think in a more comprehensive and integrated way. It doesn't make the job any simpler, it just makes it more vital and the outcomes will be better if we start to look at them in a much more comprehensive way.

While acknowledging the critical importance of this structural analysis as a foundation for their work, the groups with whom we worked also emphasized the importance of conjunctural analysis. That is to say, they pointed out the importance of the examination of the moment (conjuncture) in which they are operating — and of understanding how current forces, actors and events represent constraints or opportunities for action in the present moment. Sometimes, it is a matter of taking advantage of an unexpected opportunity: "There was a new Minister… who was looking for something to hang her hat on and we got her at the right time." And sometimes considerable study and preparation is required:

> I mean first off, you have to actually analyze [the situation]. You have to step back and analyze who holds power. And which players directly influence decision-makers who hold power. And the second thing you have to do is understand what buttons they have to push. You know, what are the interests the power holders have?… So that you're in a position to change their thinking by pressing the buttons. By understanding what their interests are and by figuring out how to deliver into those. And you can deliver into those by either withholding something they need or giving them something they need. So if they need credibility with the public you can destroy that credibility or take it away, that might be… that's a negative way of influencing them. But… you're going to be better off if you provide a mix of positive reinforcement when people do something good and negative reinforcement when people do something bad… You have to take that same type of thinking into work with either a corporation or a politician… But the first thing is to just understand who holds the power and, secondly, understand what buttons are there to press to influence the decision-makers.

The Storytellers' Foundation places considerable emphasis on reflection. According to participants, their reflective approach has had wide impact:

> What it's done is to make people start getting into reflective practice. And there's a hunger for it now, just because of modeling. So it was a very brilliant model that they planted, and it grew… That was one huge success, I would say, that affected communities, not just one person or two people.

Some activists told us that taking the time to reflect, to examine immediate experiences and events through both structural and conjunctural analysis, was important not just in developing strategies, but also because of the energizing impact of these reflections.

> It makes you go deep into what you're trying to convey and try to figure out ways that will make it come alive to other people. I enjoyed that process; we had good working sessions on how to do this. And then analyzing afterwards what worked and what didn't work. So that I find energizing.

Credibility/Reputation of the Organization

How an organization is viewed by outsiders can also be a factor in its success: "Just having our [organization's] name attached to it, I think just added more credibility to the coalition."

> One meeting I really remember clearly... the government representative's there saying to us: "Look, your message is very credible. We realize that you have better contacts and better knowledge of what is going on in that country then we do." So did that ultimately bring about change in Canadian policy is another question, but there seemed to be an understanding on the part of government people that we had our thumb on the pulse of what was going on in that particular country.

A board member from another organization reported a comment from one of their funders:

> We hear lots of really good things about you guys. We've been asking around and asking people about does your work actually make a difference. And we're hearing lots of things about how your work does make a difference.

Size may not actually matter here, as suggested by one person: "We generally hit above our weight, in terms of our advocacy. The international people that I communicate with, they don't have any clue how small we are." For others, the credibility of age and gender is used to advantage, as with the Raging Grannies:

> [The] young people that are largely engaged in these things... are easily dismissed by the establishment... It's not as easy to dismiss what [we] are about... We may look... we are, in fact, older, supposedly wiser women — and if we're engaged in whatever it is, it helps to give it some credibility.

Credibility-related effectiveness is implied in other, less direct, ways — for example, invitations from other organizations to participate in activities or campaigns or being consulted for their expertise.

> We were busy, and usually being busy here means that people are inviting you to speak to them. So, as a result, I guess in that way, I felt that we were being reasonably effective.

In another activist's words:

> It is always [our organization] that is invited to come and present the model and talk to the municipal government and everything. And why do they do that? Because they know it's [our] initiative around the world.

Some organizations are valued for their services or advice: "Companies look at us and say 'these folks can provide me with a core set of services in a way that no other consultancy can do.'"

Achieving credibility while maintaining an advocacy role is, as one outsider puts it, to be in "a very sweet spot."

> [The organization has] gained a valuable position right now in their positioning, such that they're seen as being credible by both the industry, whom they work for and against, and by the public, whom often they work for and against. And that's a very, very unique position that they hold. There are very few... groups that sit in that role. They found a very sweet spot.

Group Functioning/Effectiveness

Many of the activists considered aspects of their own groups' functioning as important contributors to success. Effective leadership, for example, "encourage[s] staff to prioritize and actually take things off the plate " or "support[s] the unleashing of energies and creativity." Referring to how staff in the Youth Project operate, a young person observed:

> They kind of sit back and watch and they give their say every once in a while. Like if something is a little too edgy, they'll totally step in and be "Yeah, maybe we should take it back a notch." And everyone kind of [says] "Okay, yeah maybe we should." So they're kind of there as facilitators, basically. We pretty much run everything.

With good communication, "Everybody knew what [others were] doing." "There's a lot of creative tension and good dialogue back and forth as we're developing policy positions" and "transparency in the sense that people's concerns could be brought up and discussed, so that it could move forward."

A related factor is organizational agility. This requires certain personal and organizational characteristics: "[Our organization] is very adaptive... I find it the most quickly and easily adapting organization I've ever worked for." This need for agility can be challenging,

> This organization is quite comfortable with uncertainty. Which is rare. I mean it's rare for individuals; it's kind of rare also particularly for institutions. And you know it takes a personal toll... We're kind of always living on the razor's edge, and it can be very difficult also for people who don't like to be in that space all the time. It can be a very sort of stressful, frustrating place to work, because it's not always clear where we're going, what we've achieved, what's happened. But I think it's interesting... in

> the sense that a lot of what we advocate for, a lot of the kinds of solutions that we would like to see, require people to be more comfortable with uncertainty.

And good humour helps. In one incident,

> Inevitably, it didn't go according to plan, so there was sort of the laughter and the adjusting, in order to make sure that [the materials] all got prepared at the right time and got out to people as was planned.

Many also identified the importance of excellent planning and organization of activities — and of clarity in policies and roles and on how decisions are made and tasks and responsibilities are delegated — as essential features of successful activist organizations. A diversity of backgrounds and skills among participants was identified as an asset by most organizations: "Just such a wide variety of, not only life experiences, but skill sets. And excellent job of utilizing those skill sets. So that's been a real positive experience."

> Within the area we concentrate… we have a huge amount of depth. So we have both technical depth, as well as having communication, as well as education depth. And we have engineering and economics and political sciences… all at our disposal.

Attracting, Engaging and Retaining Participants

Activists report that a welcoming and supportive environment helps to keep them engaged.

> A huge factor is the support that the members give to each other in whatever they happen to be doing. Since I joined, it's clear to me that my own level of energy and my own ability to tackle social actions and justice issues have been greater as a result of being part of the group and feeling the support of the larger group.

Mentoring is valued, especially by new group members.

> I was new and [my team leader's] guidance during this time… in terms of how to interact with the organization, how to go about getting decisions made and getting them made quickly. How to go about putting pressure on the right areas to make sure that things were getting done, decisions were being made, money was getting out the door, people were booking their travel. I mean that was really, really vital to have that guidance for me.

Some mentioned their organizations as havens in an otherwise potentially dangerous or unfriendly world:

> When you're not always watching your back about being called a name, or with the threat of physical violence, which is what a lot of youth face because they're coming from a lot of dangers because of who they are, or who they want to be.

Flexibility in terms of the nature and extent of the individual's involvement tends to attract participants and keep them engaged,

> It's the type of organization that gives you the capacity to get involved at whatever level you wish... So as a result, it grew into other roles and that is what brought me in to where I am now.

as do opportunities for learning and training. One person said she was attracted to Montreal's Social Justice Committee for these reasons: "You have many opportunities as a volunteer to be trained at different levels, to learn a lot." A budding teacher declared:

> Everything I know about teaching in a way that makes students want to learn and be involved and be interactive, I've learned through my experience in this organization. Things I've learned about formalizing my idea and being clear and to the point in a public speaking context, I've learned through this organization. Issues of community organization, that has been a major learning for me in this organization. And how important it is, the personal touch is, in terms of community organization... And I've learned about the power of people through here, to make a difference and to change things and to really push forward.

Methods and Strategies

The activists described a range of approaches, methods and strategies that "work" for them, including certain operating principles.

Impeccable Research

Members of one organization explain that they consistently approach issues with what they describe as an "ideologically neutral" lens that they believe is critical to what they do.

> We address issues on a case-by-case basis and based on the best available information. We tend to operate in that gray zone, as opposed to black and white. Until something happens, we can't necessarily say which side we're going to end up on.

According to its members, the "neutral" stance is critical to their credibility. This high credibility then opens doors, enabling the organization to have a voice in arenas in which they believe they can have the biggest influence. Neutrality also means their partnerships shift from issue to issue — the organization "reserves the right to disagree" with other advocacy groups depending on their analysis of any given situation. Rather than being identified in either general public awareness or policy making circles with one or another ideological perspective, this group believes its neutrality contributes to its reputation as an organization committed to problem solving.

Accompaniment, Ally or Empowerment Approaches

From these perspectives, meaningful and lasting social change is likely to be achieved only when members of marginalized groups are supported to make changes on their own behalf. As one member of the Youth Project commented,

> I think it's really brilliant, because [staff members] don't have to be there. The wisdom is inside the participants and they've devised a way of the participants pulling their own wisdom out to support each other. And it's had a huge, huge effect.

This kind of approach is of particular importance to people associated with the Disability Action Hall, who see themselves as accompanying, not directing, the work of the Hall's self advocates (members).

> The self-advocates within the Hall, by the very act of claiming a voice for themselves... that in itself is a transformative action in our society. Rather than accepting what the mainstream would [assign them] as a role of marginalization, of "Just stay in your homes, don't raise a fuss," instead, self-advocates are outside saying "No." However hard it is to be a marginalized person speaking up for themselves in this society, it's worth doing.

Collaborative Strategies

Members of all groups participating identified collaborations, networks and coalitions as critical to accomplishing their ends. Coalitions and networks are highly valued for their contributions to maximizing resources, enhancing strategic positioning, mutual support and validation and for broadening the range of alternative approaches to advancing social and environmental justice issues.

Most advocacy groups/organizations are constantly engaged in "network development" as an overall strategy regardless of the specific current goal or campaign.

> [We] didn't even necessarily need to be taking action on the issue, but just having the discussion. I think that's important — creating spaces in order to build those relationships and open the door for communication and linkages is important.

"Strong relationships" within the community were identified as "the reason the Storytellers' Foundation has been able to move forward with their work." These relationships are credited as "what's bringing people back to keep addressing issues."

Sometimes these are long-term strategic alliances, and sometimes they are "one-off" collaborations: "Here was an agency that was, in part, against what we were doing around Kraft, but who were ready to join with us in lobbying to have Canada rejoin the International Coffee Organization."

A more informal kind of collaborative relationship was also identified as important:

> To see policy change, you need to have allies inside government… [with] civil servants, politicians or usually both. And you have to build your relationships with these people so that there's trust. And when I say allies, I don't mean formal alliances, I mean sympathetic. People who understand the issue and want to help move it forward.

Some participants described collaborations among advocacy groups that entailed organizations adopting distinct positions relative to particular social justice issues. This strategy was deliberately used to create contrasts so that some positions would be seen by policy makers and the general public as more radical and others — in contrast — as more moderate. Within a conservative political environment, this strategy was used in the hopes of constructing socially progressive perspectives or positions as "moderate" and therefore more palatable.

Education/Information Strategies
As with collaboration, educational strategies were almost universally mentioned as fundamental tools, and conversations about public education unearthed a vast and inspiring array of strategies and tactics. These ranged from ongoing efforts to educate their own members and the general public about issues, to ensuring policy makers had accurate and up-to-date analysis of social and/or environmental issues. The first — educating members — was described by Alberta social workers as an important means by which to enable members to engage in social action during political campaigns. The latter — providing analyses to policy makers with the intent of achieving changes in policy or law — was mentioned by several groups as being aided in its effectiveness by the credibility of their group, and through the skill with which this is carried out.

> I shift my rhetoric down from ranting. It's more effective, I think, to provide full information and let people who are listening to or reading whatever you have to say to be treated with some respect and give them the information and expect that they will travel with you to shared conclusions.

An important part of this is to "have that research done. Having it translated into policy papers, and then having that taken and turned into neat, sharp, targeted campaigning work."

Public education strategies considered to be effective included the use of various forms of media, such as blogging, news releases and websites. Opportunities for people to tell their own stories of marginalization and empowerment were seen as powerful tools, as were other creative strategies:

> The Social Justice Committee does a whole analysis of Third World debt… through a dinner theatre. They had different tables for different people. So different people ate different things. Some people ate almost nothing, even though you paid for a meal.

Some groups developed strategies specifically designed to increase the likelihood of attention from local news media. These may involve purposively creating spectacles to draw public and media attention. Other organizations take what might be characterized as more "professional" approaches to attracting media attention, such as providing accessible analyses of complex social, political or environmental issues.

Clear Focus

Being deliberate in how the organization uses its resources — in terms of time, energy or money — was mentioned repeatedly as a critical facilitator of success. Many groups believe that success is more likely when efforts are focused on only one or a few issues. One activist noted it was "absolutely" important to "set up very, very, very few priorities and everybody working around that." Another explained why the group was at its best when the focus was on one issue:

> Because then you've got all of the resources brought to bear. You've got people's attention, you've got people's time carved out. You know something has been prioritized, either by the organization or by external events, so that you've got... buy-in from your volunteers and from your members across the country.

For the Youth Project, it's important that the focus be on issues identified by the youth themselves. While this may seem an obvious strategy, one participant implied that it can also be difficult, as he described the group being most effective when they "remember what is important, and don't get caught up in personalities or egos. So you remember what's important. You just sort of take the blows and keep going."

Careful Preparation

In addition to the upfront and ongoing careful analysis of the context and of opportunities for action, careful planning and preparation for the range of activities associated with their work was consistently identified as a key facilitator of success. This includes the judicious use of resources. Frequent mention was made of how important it is that groups both use and celebrate the individual talents and strengths of members, whether in the form of special knowledge, grant writing skills or creativity in approaches to activist practice. The use of individual talents and strengths is seen as not only contributing to goal achievement, but also as energy-building as individuals feel recognized and valued for their unique contributions.

Sometimes activists speak also in terms of making best use of the strengths of the organization itself. For example, in a strategic partnership that capitalized on the strengths of each group,

> They are the ones who... have the research capacity, the information, the savvy of

what's going on internally. So we collaborate with them. What we have is people power and we [are] savvy about campaigning and getting the message out in a popular way.

Developing and Presenting Solutions

According to many of the activists with whom we spoke, presenting solutions rather than criticisms is a strategy that facilitates success because providing recommendations for positive change helps avoid the "troublemaker" label. This approach says: "This is the problem. This is the solution. And this is how you can be part of that solution." Being "solution-focused" is seen as a way to engage a particular audience with a solution. Policy makers, for example, may want more detailed recommendations while the media may be more likely to prefer brief, straightforward messages that are easily and quickly understood. If it is the general public whose help is being enlisted to solve a problem, as in Oxfam's "Fair Trade in Coffee" campaign, activists stress the importance of finding meaningful but accessible ways people can contribute.

Tenacity

Many of the activists emphasized the extent to which success depends on persistence. "Change is slow," there are "many roadblocks" and you have to "find a way to get around everything." Nevertheless,

> Keep going back. It's easy to get discouraged and quit… after you've been told "no" a number of times… Also knowing when to say okay, we need to leave this one for a while, before we go back at it.

Creativity

> I've seen things being tried and then been taken away, because, "Okay, we tried it. That's not going to work. Let's take it back to the drawing board." I've seen a lot of ideas come in and out. And I've seen a lot of ideas come and stay.

Humour

For many activists, a sense of humour was fundamental — especially in the context of risk-taking and the need to for tenacity. For many, good humour is just necessary for hanging in there with the work. According to one person, "you have that sort of work hard, play hard kind of personality quite a bit." For others (such as the Raging Grannies and the Youth Project), the use of humour was a specific strategy in their work.

What Works: A Note on Using Appreciative Inquiry Tools

In a conference presentation related to this project we were asked why, in collaborating with activist groups, we would be "using the tools of the oppressor" — Appreciative Inquiry, which originated in the organizational development/management literature. In addition to this critique, appreciative inquiry is sometimes disparaged on the grounds that it "only focuses on the positive."

Having reflected on these criticisms — as well as on indications in the literature that AI tools tend to be energizing to groups — prior to undertaking this project, it was our judgment that these might be of value to the activist groups.[4] With respect to the "only the positive" criticism, it seemed to us that the "dream" phase of AI — in our interview protocol asking people to visualize a desired future (and how they might get there) — clearly addresses this issue. In the gap between the current situation and an ideal future, "deficits" are unquestionably implicit. This method simply focuses not on the negative, but on how to get to a positive future.

Our experience of this process was that the focus on the groups' successes was, as the literature suggests, energizing for the groups — helping to animate people to take on the challenge of addressing the gap between where they are and where they want to be.

Notes

1. This was identified as an even more complex issue by groups with funders to whom they are accountable.
2. For some this means engagement of the wider citizenry; for others it refers to their own membership.
3. Attributed to Emma Goldman based on a passage in her *Living My Life* (1931: 56): "I did not believe that a Cause which stood for a beautiful ideal, for anarchism, for release and freedom from convention and prejudice, should demand the denial of life and joy."
4. In fact, several of these groups had previous experience with AI.

12

SENSE MAKING

LESSONS FROM SUCCESS STORIES

Elizabeth Whitmore, Avery Calhoun and Maureen G. Wilson

> Success is such a funny thing. I think through this work, I've really changed my idea of what success is. I don't know if numbers really measure it so well… Someone was saying that it's like the ripple effect, you know? That one drop might not do anything, but the ripple eventually is going to hit something, and change something. So it's really hard to say whether something has been successful or not, because people are so complex and it takes so much time for change to become apparent.

This project gave us a rare opportunity to interact with a variety of activists to explore their ideas about effectiveness, and about what contributes to achieving success. We've heard their stories and views in individual interviews, workshops, a symposium, and in the chapters written by activists for this book. In their work to correct injustices, we have seen admirable creativity and insight.

There is a widespread belief among these activists in the value and importance of the engagement of citizens in challenging injustices, and in actively participating in shaping their world. The assumption that ordinary people can develop what Freire called "critical consciousness" — to see beyond their personal experiences of the world to understand the power relationships that created our reality — underlies much of the work that has been described in this book.

Ideas matter in social change, and it matters whose ideas dominate. Each of these activist groups, in resonance with Gramsci's views on the importance of the question of ideological hegemony (the War of Ideas), dedicates a part of its work to contesting dominant societal ideas. These efforts, directed at raising awareness or changing attitudes among the general public, and specific target groups (such as politicians or other decision makers), include a wide range of strategies — providing solid research and working hard to inform and reframe public policy debates, developing educational materials, holding public forums and rallies and using the media to convey information and opinions.[1]

The engagement of citizens, including engagement of people in their own groups, is a matter of importance to all of the groups partnering with us. This concern is not just with numbers alone, but with who those people are. There is an aspiration to reach and engage a broad and diverse spectrum of people, including "the mainstream." The quality of that engagement is important as well, as activists told us they value civility, nonviolence, collaboration, risk-taking and just the fact that people are "standing up and making themselves heard."

People have told us that the credibility and workings of their groups can have important impacts on how well they do. With whom credibility is important of course varies with each group. Aspects of organizational functioning said to be significant included: open and participatory leadership; organizational agility; clarity in policies, roles and decision-making processes; excellent planning and organization of activities; good internal communication; diversity of participant backgrounds and skills; and, universally, a culture encouraging a sense of humour. Groups said they had learned that people's participation was attracted and retained by the presence of energy and enthusiasm, by a welcoming and supportive environment, by mentoring and opportunities for learning and training and by flexibility in terms of the nature and extent of the individual's involvement.

The personal experience of engagement in activism can be powerful. This is often expressed as related to a feeling of "being a part of something bigger" or of "being together with people who share the same vision and commitment." Feeling a part of something bigger gives hope of change that could not be achieved by an individual alone; wanting to see change and joining others who share that passion can be an exhilarating experience. This is accompanied by important learning — about issues, about strategies and about oneself. For people with personal identification with a group's cause, the activist group can be a haven in a dangerous and unfriendly world. And as shame and isolation are replaced by pride and a sense of community, these can morph into a shift of focus from the personal to the political and a politicized involvement in the fight for social justice. At its best, this work is done in the energizing context of lots of laughter, music, food and fun.

Trying to bring about social change can be discouraging uphill work. While it is unquestionably true that when a specific concrete objective has been met, people are heartened in their desire to carry on "doing the right thing," it may be that other things are even more important in keeping activists going.

Many activist groups struggle with questions of accountability. We share their frustration with linear thinking based in the language of prediction, measurability and control, which simply doesn't work when dealing with the "messiness of real life" (Zimmerman 2000). Woodhill (2009: 6) describes the source of this dilemma:

> The great success of the biophysical sciences in understanding the natural world and being able to use this understanding for prediction and technological development has tricked us. It has led us to believe that this sort of logic and analysis is "best" and if we can simply apply it to the worlds of economics, social relations and politics, we will be better at managing, controlling and developing our organizations, communities and societies.

In trying to free ourselves of what Woodhill (2009: 6) calls "a hangover of linear thinking" and to essentially reframe the discussion, we have found ourselves exploring the potential in complexity theory,[2] which resonated more fully with our experience in that it "provided the language and models to explain our intuitive actions" (Zimmerman 2000: 1).

Complexity Theory: Helping Make Sense of the Dynamics of Success

At a May 2010 conference on complexity[3] a colleague from India asked: "So what's new about complexity? We live it every day." The implied skepticism is echoed in Chambers' questions: "Whose complexity counts? And who counts complexity?" (cited in Patton 2010: 122). These questions invite us to make careful use of complexity thinking, trying to avoid the implication that it provides any kind of panacea and keeping in mind that, like other sense-making devices, there could be dangers that it might be useful for some people at the expense of others.

Until recently, most of us have been encouraged to understand our worlds through a "systems as machines" metaphor. We've been steeped in linear, mechanistic ways of thinking, and have planned campaigns and programs believing that we should be able to predict and measure results or outcomes. Complexity thinking invites us to change the metaphor from "systems as machines" to "systems as living entities." This opens up our thinking, challenging us to see what other questions we can ask (Zimmerman 2000). Though complexity thinking is vast, multidisciplinary and rapidly expanding, "it is only starting to shape thinking in the social, economic and political realms" (Ramalingam and Jones 2008: 24). In the field of evaluation, Patton characterizes complexity as "the great unexplored frontier" (2010: 1), and complexity and complexity theory are emerging as themes in discussions of action research (Dick 2009; Phelps and Hase 2002; Radford 2007).

Complexity is not a single theory but rather a loose network of ideas, a set of mental models (Rosenhead 1998). It provides a bridge among disciplines, with the study of life (biology) as a connecting glue (Zimmerman 2000). It includes a number of key concepts:

- Actions or elements are assumed to be 'interconnected and interdependent.' That is, the relationships among parts or actors are critical such that, rather than looking for measureable outcomes or particular results, awareness is attuned to patterns and connections between events or issues.
- "Uncertainty, unpredictability and ambiguity" are inevitable aspects of systems. Systems are always shifting and evolving. Small changes can make a huge difference to what happens next. Change is thus perpetual, which means that adapting is constantly required. Human agency plays a central role, however. What people do can make a difference. "While complex systems cannot be fully controlled, the directions in which they evolve can be influenced" (Woodhill 2009: 8). Operating on the edge of chaos, we search for the order underlying the seemingly random behaviours of complex systems. This can be "a region of highly creative energy" (Zimmerman 2000: 3).
- "Diversity," in terms of approaches to thinking, is key to innovation, adaptation and sustainability. This relates to the concepts of "emergence" (behaviour emerging from the self organizing interaction among the parts) and "attractors" (patterns or areas that draw the energy of the system to them). Rather than focus on resistance to change, it is more productive to use the natural energy of the system to support change. Using a complexity framework also helps us move toward "both/and" rather than "either/or" ways of thinking (Ramalingen and Jones 2008; Zimmerman 2000).
- Complex systems are "context specific." There are no models or generalizations that can easily transfer across environments, but one can learn from the experience of others. In complex environments it is more useful to value reflection and to think of good practices rather than best practices. In the international development field, Rihani (2002) concludes that success or failure depends on what is, or is not, done locally (see also Patton 2010).

The Cynefin framework (Snowdon and Boone 2007) can be helpful in clarifying our understanding of the contexts in which we are operating.

In simple situations, assessing effectiveness is quite straightforward; for example, one counts how many times something happened or measures the difference before and after an intervention. Stability and clear cause and effect relationships are easily discernible by everyone. People assess the facts of a situation, categorize them and respond based on established practice.

"Best practices" are established and it is assumed that what worked in one context will work in another.

In a complicated context, there may be more than one right answer. This takes more thought and therefore experts are often called upon to analyze a situation and look at the pros and cons of different options. Good practices, rather than best practices, are more appropriate here.

Complex situations are unpredictable and in constant flux. There is no right answer; rather, over time, patterns can be discerned and a path forward emerges. Thus, one first probes for information, senses patterns and only then responds, always ready for the next adaptation. In complex contexts, there are many opportunities for creativity and innovation.

In chaotic situations, searching for right answers is pointless. There is no time for input; someone must take charge and decide what to do. The most important thing is to act immediately to "stop the bleeding" and establish some kind of order. While being in the midst of chaos can be a good place for innovation, as people may be more than usually open to novelty, it can also prompt authoritarian leadership and stagnation once the crisis has passed (Snowdon and Boone 2007).

As with the quotation opening this chapter, these concepts resonate with the experience of individual stories of and interviews and discussions with our project partners, who have difficulty putting their sense of effectiveness into simple cause-effect terms and pointing to outcomes that could be readily measured. Understanding the vital interconnectedness of their work, illustrated in the ubiquitous presence of networks, coalitions and collabora-

The Cynefin Framework

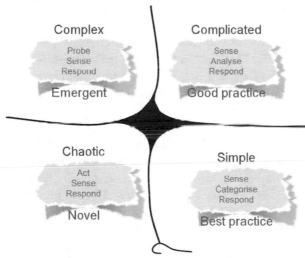

Dave Snowdon photo

tions among organizations, they are well aware that unpredictability is part of the process, and that learning and adapting is ongoing. To us, it seems that activists are often most excited and feel most creative when they were operating "on the edge of chaos."

We realized that the use of AI helps to focus on emergence and attractors, as we probed activists' stories for deeper meaning. We each make sense in unique and creative ways. Our challenge or, rather, opportunity, is to embrace this ambiguity and find ways to release the energy, commitment and enthusiasm of activists and the attractors in our work that support progressive change.

Making Sense of Activism

In reflecting on the stories of success we have heard, it seems to us then that complexity thinking might be useful in helping us to make sense of what we have heard. It would be possible, for instance, to track the emergence of critical events and engage those involved in understanding the significance and generate ideas about possible responses. Using complexity as a perspective would put the focus on emergent patterns and relationships and we could think about success in more creative ways. Rather than looking for predetermined causes or results, we would be open to looking for "surprises," things we wouldn't have expected based on our (perhaps unacknowledged) underlying assumptions about what effectiveness means and how it might relate to things activists hoped might trigger it. Surprises tell us about our implicit and explicit assumptions, bringing those into awareness and therefore providing opportunities for reflection (Guijt 2008).

Understanding the distinctions among simple, complicated, complex and chaotic contexts and how these shape practice might help us to understand the dynamics involved in the experiences reported by activist groups and organizations. Most operate in complex contexts and even sometimes in chaotic ones; rarely do they find themselves in simple situations. These are not absolute or discrete categories — a given situation may, in fact, contain elements of all four (simple, complicated, complex and chaotic). Wise activists tailor their approaches to the complexity of the circumstances they face (Patton 2010: 108).

By proactively looking for and welcoming surprises, we are empowered to learn and adapt to shifting circumstances. The activist stories in this volume exemplify this dynamic; success was enhanced as people learned and adapted as situations shifted. Westley, Zimmerman and Patton reinforce this in their discussion of social innovators and complexity, concluding that "social activists can use the insights that come from complexity theory to increase the likelihood of success" (2006: 21). In fact, much of this is congruent with what we actually did in the workshops, and later the symposium associated with this project; here we might have an example of a situation in which complexity theory "provided the language and models to explain our intuitive actions" (Zimmerman 2000: 1).

Making Meaning: Stories, Reflection and the Problem of Accountability

While we will all make sense of topics raised in this book in our own ways, take lessons from the stories and make decisions based on the fit with our own contexts, we would like to draw attention to several issues that seem especially relevant to us in complex contexts.

The Potential in Narrative

> Stories are vital to us because the primary way we process information is through *induction* [emphasis in original]… We like stories because they feed our inductive thinking machine, they give us material to find patterns in — stories are a way in which we learn. (Beinhocker 2005: 126-127, cited in Guijt 2008: 226)

Or, put more succinctly, "The stories are the point" (Patton 2010: xii).

Exploring activist success by using stories has been valuable in our project in several ways. Stories encouraged our participants to first describe specific incidents when talking about success. Stories take us "somewhere else," bringing an experience alive in its detail and often intense vividness. Stories touch us at both cognitive and emotional levels, surfacing both content and feelings in relation to an experience. Because of their evocativeness, stories helped us to "enter" the experience with our partners, allowing us to build empathy as we could feel the excitement together. Learning is about relationships, and stories are one way to create those connections. Guijt suggests that learning through story-telling is also a democratic process: "By clarifying understanding, those involved are acting to create meaning" (2008: 226). The stories people told provided a basis for probing for deep levels of understanding and analysis. Thus interviews helped both "interviewer" and "interviewee" make sense of what we were hearing and experiencing, to find connections or patterns between events, actions and people, and their thoughts and feelings.

Bornstein writes of the role of stories in creating impetus for change. The belief that one can change the world

> does not emerge suddenly. The capacity to cause change grows in an individual over time as small scale efforts lead gradually to larger ones. But the process needs a beginning — a story, an example, an early taste of success — something along the way that helps a person form the belief that it is possible to make the world a better place. Those who act on that belief spread it to others. They are

> highly contagious. Their stories must be told. (2007: 290-291, cited
> in Patton 2010: 146)

The Importance of Reflection

> For fast acting relief, try slowing down. (Lily Tomlin)

Taking time to reflect on the systems in which we operate is, sadly, usually considered a luxury (Menzies 2005). Many activists described time for reflection as a desperate need and the lack of it a source of frustration. Some organizations do manage to build in processes such as reflecting (Storytellers) or debriefing (Pembina, Youth Project) into the routine of their work. Yet one of the most important implications of complexity science, according to Ramalingam and Jones is that "it provides ways for practitioners, policy makers, leaders, managers and researchers [to] all stop and collectively reflect on how we are thinking about trying to solve problems" (2008: 65). We see, in the stories of activists, that reflection can and does happen, though it is rarer than any of us would like. Patton (2010) argues that reflective practice is not only essential to understanding what's going on in an emergent process and, more importantly, its implications, but also deepens relationships among too often disconnected participants.

Contribution Rather than Attribution

Many organizations are called upon by funders as well as the public for measurable outcomes of their activities in the name of accountability. Yet most work in constantly changing circumstances and in collaboration with others, so attributing any outcome to one group or activity would rarely be accurate. Referring to the lack of resources to examine the uncertainties of their efforts when planning programs and projects, Ramalingam and Jones lament that "the pressure of accountability to donors or the public may not allow for such uncertainties to be honestly and openly addressed" (2008: 66). Activism and advocacy are complex activities, and even more so when working closely, or in parallel ways, with other groups.

Activists themselves certainly identify attribution and demands for accountability as a problem, acknowledging the impossibility of immediately knowing whether an event or action actually "causes" an outcome. Inevitably, there are many players, and many "causes."[4] They know that achieving the change for which they hope will involve "a long, slow process" and that they may never know the full results of their work. A major worry is that a reliance on measureable outcomes might "force people to choose, as advocacy targets, quantifiable things that aren't necessarily systemic change."

A shift in attitudes is needed by both organizations and funders around this issue. The concept of contribution fits far more appropriately and accurately than attribution in complex contexts. As time and resource-consuming as it may be to step back and reflect on how to address this question, it is essential if our work is to make real differences (Ramalingam and Jones 2008: 66).

Celebrating Our Work

> In the journey to social justice, small steps sometimes lead to unexpected leaps of progress. (Robert Thurman)

Again, we want to thank the activists we have had the privilege of meeting in the course of this research and who have shared their time and wisdom with us. We humbly present these thoughts as just that — some ideas about success in activist work — based on what we have learned from these remarkable people.

One of the participants urged us all to remember to celebrate:

> I actually think we're at our best [when] there's something that we've… been involved in that we have perceived [ourselves] as having won — a victory or that we've done something very well. You know we've worked together well at it, so it could be the way all parts of the organization pulled out all stops to work around the tsunami, for example. It could be when we look at some of the work that we've done around advocacy, where we've seen changes happen at a particular level — be it our own federal government, be it at the WTO level. And I think that we realize we worked hard, we were deliberate, we worked collaboratively and we achieved something… It may not have changed the world, but we achieved something that we set ourselves out to and we can celebrate it.

Notes

1. Just as the ideological hegemony of neoliberalism is incomplete and thus open to challenge, neither is corporate control of the media or other public spaces complete; opportunities do present themselves for activists to access these and other means of communicating.
2. Complexity theory derives from a number of sciences and the literature is extensive. Our discussion here draws only on some of its main features that seem most appropriate to understanding social phenomena.
3. See <cdi.wur.nl> for details.
4. Mayne (2007) offers us a six-step method in response to this problem. Though he does assume an identifiable program (rather than some of the more amorphous activities carried out by our partners) and relatively stable contexts, the method does provide a tool for activist organizations to address funder pressure to attribute outcomes to their work.

RESOURCES

FRAMEWORKS, GUIDES AND COMPLEXITY

Frameworks

California Endowment <www.calendow.org>.

Chapman, Jennifer, and Amboka Wameyo. 2001 (January). *"Monitoring And Evaluating Advocacy: A Scoping Study."* London: ActionAid. At <actionaid.org>.

Chapman, Jennifer, Almir Pereira Jr., and Valerie Miller. 2006. *"Critical Webs of Power and Change: Summary of Learning."* Working Paper One. At <actionaid.org>.

CIDA (Canadian International Development Agency). (nd). At <www.acdi-cida.gc.ca>.

DFID (Department of International Development, UK).(nd). <www.dfid.gov.uk>.

Evaluation Exchange. 2007. XIII 1. Special Issue on Evaluating Advocacy and Policy Change. At <hfrp.org/evaluation>.

Guthrie, Kendall, Justin Louie, Tom David and Catherine Crystal Foster. 2005 (October). *"The Challenge of Assessing Policy and Advocacy Activities: Strategies for a Prospective Evaluation Approach."* A study conducted for the California Endowment. At <calendow.org>.

Just Associates. nd. "What is Success? Measuring and Evaluating the Impact of Social Justice Advocacy and Citizen Organizing Strategies." At <justassociates.org>.

Kellogg Foundation. 2007. "Designing Initiative Evaluation: A Systems-oriented Framework for Evaluating Social Change Efforts." Battle Creek, MI. At <wkkf.org>.

Laraia, Barbara A., Janice Dodds, and Eugenia Eng. 2003. "A Framework for Assessing the Effectiveness of Anti-Hunger Advocacy Organizations." *Health Education and Behavior* 30, 6.

Lempert, Ted. February 2009. "An Advocate's Perspective: Ten Considerations for Effective Advocacy Evaluation." At <organizationalresearch.com>. Also available at <innonet.org>.

Patton, Michael Quinn. 2008 (March)."Advocacy Impact Evaluation." *Journal of Multidisciplinary Evaluation* 5, 9. At <plexusinstitute.org/edgeware>.

Raynor, Jared. 2009 (January 20). "Evaluating *Organizational Advocacy Capacity: A Short-Term Measure of Success.*" At <calendow.org/uploadedFiles/Evaluation/Raynor%20Advocacy%20Capacity.pdf>.

Raynor, Jared, Peter York, and Chao-Chee Sim. 2009 (January). *"What Makes an*

Effective Advocacy Organization: A Framework for Determining Advocacy Capacity?"
California Endowment. At <calendow.org>.
USAID Advocacy Framework. nd. "Appendix 2. Supporting Civic Advocacy: Strategic
Approaches For Donor-Supported Civic Advocacy Programs." (Draft version)
USAID Office of Democracy and Governance. At <usaid.gov>.
World Bank Advocacy Framework. n.d.. "Appendix 3. Community Empowerment
and Social Inclusion (CESI) Module on Participatory Planning for Advocacy,
Communication and Coalition Building." At <worldbank.org>.

Guides

Asibey, Edith. 2008. "Are We There Yet? A Communications Evaluation Guide."
At <calendow.org/uploadedFiles/Evaluation/Asibey%20Are%20We%20
There%20Yet.pdf>.
Asibey, Edith, and David Devlin-Foltz. 2007. "Continuous Progress: Better Advocacy
Through Evaluation." *The Evaluation Exchange XIII.* At <continuousprogress.
org>.
Binder-Aviles, Hilary. 2009. "Build Your Advocacy Grantmaking: Advocacy
Evaluation Tool and Advocacy Capacity Assessment Tool." At <calendow.
org/uploadedFiles/Evaluation/AFJ/Mosaica/Assessing/AdvocacyCapacity.
pdf?n=3393>.
Coffman, Julia C (2009). *A User's Guide to Advocacy Evaluation Planning.* Cambridge,
MA.
Devlin-Foltz, David. 2009a. "The Advocacy Progress Planner: An Advocacy and
Policy Change Composite Logic Model." At <calendow.org/uploadedFiles/
Evaluation/Devlin-Foltz%20APP.pdf>.
_____. 2009b. "Model benchmarks." At <calendow.org/uploadedFiles/Evaluation/
Devlin-Foltz%20Model%20APP%20Benchmarks.pdf>.
Gienapp, Anne, Jane Reisman, and Sarah Stachowiak. 2009 (August). "Getting
Started: A Self-Directed Guide to Outcome Map Development." Prepared for
the Annie E. Casey Foundation by Organizational Research Services. Seattle.
At <organizationalresearchcom>.
Innovation Network, Inc. nd. "Pathfinder: A Practical Guide to Advocacy Evaluation."
Advocates Edition. At <innonet.org/advocacy>.
Labonte, Ronald, and Joan Feather. 1996. *Handbook on Using Stories in Health Promotion
Practice.* Ottawa, ON: Health Canada.
Reisman, Jane, Anne Gienapp, and Sarah Stachowiak. 2007. "A Guide to Measuring
Advocacy And Policy." Prepared for the Annie E. Casey Foundation by
Organizational Research Services. At <organizationalresearch.com> and
<aecf.org>.
Stephens, Michael. 2009. "Toward Good Practice In Public Engagement: A
Participatory Evaluation Guide For CSOs." Ottawa: Canadian Council for
International Co-operation. At <ccic.ca>.

Complexity

Evaluation Revisited: Improving the Quality of Evaluative Practice by Embracing
Complexity (May 20 & 21, 2010: Utrecht, Netherlands). <www.cdi.wur.nl/uk/

newsagenda/archive/agenda/2010>.

Guijt, Irene. 2008. *Seeking Surprises: Rethinking Monitoring for Collective Learning in Rural Resource Management*. Wageningen, Netherlands: University of Wageningen.

Patton, Michael Quinn. 2010. *Developmental Evaluation: Applying Complexity Concepts to Enhance Innovation and Use*. New York: Guilford.

_____. 2009 (January 20). "Developmental Evaluation: Evaluating Under Conditions Of Complexity." At <calendow.org/uploadedFiles/Evaluation/Patton%20 Developmental%20Evaluation.pdf? n=8316>.

Ramalingam, Ben, and Harry Jones with Reba Toussaint and John Young. 2008. "Exploring the Science of Complexity: Ideas and Implications for Development and Humanitarian Efforts." Working Paper 285 (second edition). London: Overseas Development Institute (ODI).

Rihani, Samir. 2002. *Complexity Systems Theory and Development Practice: Understanding Non-Linear Realities*. London: Zed.

Rosenhead, Jonathan. 1998. *Complexity Theory and Management Practice*. Working Paper LSEOR 9825, London School of Economics, Operational Research (ISBN:0 7530 12537).

Snowden, David J., and Mary E. Boone. 2007. "A Leader's Framework For Decision Making." *Harvard Business Review* 85,11.

Westley, Frances, Brenda Zimmerman, and Michael Quinn Patton. 2006. *Getting to Maybe: How the World is Changed*. Toronto, ON: Random House.

Woodhill, Jim. 2009 (December). "Introduction." In Seerp Wigboldus and Mirjam Schaap (eds.), *Innovation Dialogue: Being Strategic in the Face of Complexity*. Conference report. Wageningen, The Netherlands: Wageningen UR Centre for Development Innovation. At <cdi.wur.nl/UK/>.

Zimmerman, Brenda. 2000. "A Complexity Science Primer: What is Complexity Science and Why Should I Learn About It?" At <plexusinstitute.com/edge-ware>.

SELECT BIBLIOGRAPHY

Adler, Barbara. 2009. "The Accordian." Presentation at Symposium. Hazelton, BC. <www.badler.ca>.

Advocacy Evaluation Project. n.d. At <innonet.org/advocacy>.

Alberta Royalty Review Panel. 2007. "Our Fair Share: Report of the Alberta Royalty Review Panel." (September 18).

Alger, Charles F. 1997. "Transnational Social Movements, World Politics and Global Governance." In Jackie Smith, Charles Chatfield, and Ron Pugnucco (eds.), *Transnational Social Movements and Global Politics: Solidarity Beyond the State*. Syracuse, NY: Syracuse University Press.

Alinsky, Saul. 1969. *Reveille for Radicals*. New York: Vintage Books.

Alliance for Justice. 2005. *Build Your Advocacy Grantmaking: Advocacy Evaluation Tool*. Washington, DC. At <afj.org>.

Anand, Sudhir, and Paul Segal. 2009. "What Do We Know about Global Income Inequality?" In Sudhir Anand, Paul Segal and Joseph Stiglitz (eds.), *Debates in the Measurement of Global Poverty*. New York: Oxford University Press.

Asibey, Edith. 2008. "Are We There Yet? A Communications Evaluation Guide." At <calendow.org/uploadedFiles/Evaluation/Asibey%20Are%20We%20There%20Yet.pdf>.

Asibey, Edith, and David Devlin-Foltz. 2007. "Continuous Progress: Better Advocacy through Evaluation." *The Evaluation Exchange XIII*. At <continuousprogress.org>.

Bagnell Stuart, Jennifer. 2007. "Evaluations to Watch: Necessity Leads to Innovative Evaluation Approach and Practice" *The Evaluation Exchange* XIII, 1.

Barlow, Connie (ed.). 1992. *From Gaia to Selfish Genes: Selected Writings in the Life Sciences*. Cambridge: MIT Press.

Bastien, Betty. 2004. *Blackfoot Ways of Knowing: The Worldview of the Siksikaitsitapi*. Calgary, AB: University of Calgary Press.

Berger, Peter L., and Thomas Luckman. 1966. *The Social Construction of Reality*. New York: Anchor Books.

Beukema, Leni, and Ben Valkenburg. 2007. "Demand-Driven Elderly Care in the Netherlands." *Action Research* 5(2): 1610180.

Binder-Aviles, Hilary. 2009. "Build Your Advocacy Grantmaking: Advocacy Evaluation Tool and Advocacy Capacity Assessment Tool." At <calendow.org/uploadedFiles/Evaluation/AFJ/Mosaica/Assessing/AdvocacyCapacity.pdf?n=3393>.

Boaz, Annette, and Carol Hayden. 2002. "Pro-Active Evaluators: Enabling Research to Be Useful, Usable and Used." *Evaluation* 8, 4.

Brinkerhoff, Robert O. 2003. *The Success Case Method*. San Francisco: Berrett Koehler.

Brown, Leslie, and Susan Strega. 2005. "Transgressive Possibilities." In Leslie Brown and Susan Strega (eds.), *Research as Resistance: Critical, Indigenous and Anti-Oppressive Approaches*. Toronto, ON: Canadian Scholars' Press.

Brown, L. David, Gabrielle Bammer, Batliwala Srilatha, and Frances Kunreuther. 2003. "Framing Practice-Research Engagement for Democratizing Knowledge." *Action Research* 1(1): 81–102.

Brydon-Miller, Mary, Davydd Greenwood, and Patricia Maguire. 2003. "Why Action Reseach." *Action Research* 1(1): 9–28. <http://www.civitas.edu.pl/pub/nasza_uczelnia/projekty_badawcze/Taylor/Brydon-Miller.pdf>

Bushe, Gervase R. 1998. "Appreciative Inquiry with Teams." *Organization Development Journal* 16(3): 41.

Calgary Sun. 2006. "Simply Bizarre." Calgary, AB: Author. July 13.

Cameron, Duncan. 1996 (August). "Mad Economists' Disease." *The Canadian Forum*.

Campbell, Marie, and Frances Gregor. 2002. *Mapping Social Relations*. Toronto, ON: Garamond.

Canadian Association of Social Workers. 2005. "Code of Ethics and Guidelines for Ethical Practice." <http://www.casw-acts.ca>.

Capra, Fritjof. 1996. "The Web of Life." *Resurgence* 178.

CARE International. 2008. "Living on the Edge of Emergency: Paying the Price of Inaction." At <reliefweb/int/rw/lib.nsf/db900SID/SHIG-7JLCMK?OpenDocument>.

Carmichael, Kevin. 2010. "New World Order." *Globe and Mail*. February 6.

Carroll, William K. 2006. "Marx's Method and the Contributions of Institutional Ethnography." In Caelie Frampton, Gary Kinsman, AK Thompson and Kate Tilliczek (eds.), *Sociology for Changing the World: Social Movements/Social Research*. Halifax: Fernwood Publishing.

Chambers, Robert. 2005. *Ideas For Development*. London: Earthscan.

Change Agency. nd. "Advocacy Progress Planner." At <thechangeagency.org>.

Chapman, Jennifer. 2002. "Monitoring and Evaluating Advocacy." *PLA Notes* 43.

Chapman, Jennifer, Almir Pereira Jr., and Valerie Miller. 2006. "Critical Webs of Power and Change: Summary of Learning." Working Paper One. At <action-aid.org>.

Chapman, Jennifer, and Amboka Wameyo. 2001 (January). "Monitoring and Evaluating Advocacy: A Scoping Study." London: ActionAid. At <actionaid.org>.

Chossudovsky, Michel. 2003. *The Globalization of Poverty and the New World Order*. Ottawa: Global Research.

Chovanec, Donna M., Elizabeth A. Lange, and Lee C. Ellis. 2008. "Social Movement Learning: A Catalyst for Action." In Marie Hammond-Callaghan and Matthew Hayday (eds.), *Mobilizations, Protests and Engagements: Canadian Perspectives on Social Movements*. Halifax: Fernwood Publishing.

CIDA (Canadian International Development Agency). (nd). At <www.acdi-cida.gc.ca>.

Cisneros-Puebla, 2007. "The Deconstructive and Reconstructive Faces of Social Construction. Kenneth Gergen in Coversation with César A. Cisneros-Puebla." *Qualitative Social Research* 9, 1. At <qualitative-research.net/fqs-texte/1-08/08-1-20-3.htm>.

Coates, Barry, and David Osalind. 2002. "Learning from Change: The Art of Assessing the Impact of Advocacy Work." *Development and Practice* 12, 3 and 4.

Coffman, Julia. 2009 (January). *Framing Paper: Current Advocacy Evaluation Practice.* Los Angeles, CA: The California Endowment.

_____. 2009. "A User's Guide to Advocacy Evaluation Planning." Cambridge, MA: Harvard Family Research Project. At <innonet.org>.

_____. 2007. "What's Different About Evaluating Advocacy and Policy Change?" *The Evaluation Exchange* XIII, 1.

Coffman, Julia, and Ehren Reed. 2009. "Unique Methods in Advocacy Evaluation." At <calendow.org/uploadedFiles/Evaluation/Coffman%20Reed%20 Unique%20Methods%20%28paper%29.pdf>.

Coleman, James S. 1988. "Social Capital in the Creation of Human Capital." *The American Journal of Sociology* 94, S1. (Supplement: Organizations and Institutions: Sociological and Economic Approaches to the Analysis of Social Structure).

Conway, Janet M. 2004. *Identity, Place, Knowledge: Social Movements Contesting Globalization.* Halifax: Fernwood Publishing.

Cooke, Bill, and Julie Cox. 2005. *Fundamentals of Action Research.* Four volumes. London: Sage.

Cooperrider, David L., Frank Barrett, and Suresh Srivastava. 1995. "Social Construction and Appreciative Inquiry: A Journey in Organizational Theory." In David Hosking, H. Peter Dachler, and Kenneth Gergen (eds.), *Management and Organization: Relational Alternatives to Individualism.* Aldershot, UK: Avebury Press.

Cooperrider, David L., and Diana Whitney. 1999. "A Positive Revolution in Change: Appreciative Inquiry." The Taos Institute <www.appreciativeinquiry.case. edu>.

Cooperrider, David L., Dawn Whitney, and Jacqueline M. Stavros (eds.). 2003. *Appreciative Inquiry Handbook: The First in a Series of AI Workbooks for Leaders of Change.* San Francisco, CA: Berrett-Koehler.

Crutchfield, Leslie, and Heather McLeod Grant. 2008. *Forces for Good: The Six Practices of High-Impact Nonprofits.* San Francisco: John Wiley & Sons.

Davies, Rick. 2001 (August). *Evaluating the Effectiveness of DFID's Influence With Multilaterals. Part A: A Review of NGO Approaches to the Evaluation of Advocacy Work.* London, UK: Actionaid Impact Assessment Unit.

Denzin, Norman K., and Yvonna S. Lincoln. 2005. "Introduction: The Discipline and Practice of Qualitative Research." In Norman K. Denzin and Yvonna S. Lincoln (eds.), *The Sage Handbook of Qualitative Research.* Thousand Oaks, CA: Sage.

Desmarais, Annette Aurélie. 2007. *La Vía Campesina: Globalization and the Power of Peasants.* Halifax and London: Fernwood Publishing and Pluto Press:

Devlin-Foltz, David. 2009a. "The Advocacy Progress Planner: An Advocacy and Policy Change Composite Logic Model." At <calendow.org/uploadedFiles/ Evaluation/Devlin-Foltz%20APP.pdf>.

_____. 2009b. "Model Benchmarks." At <calendow.org/uploadedFiles/Evaluation/

Devlin Foltz%20Model%20APP%20Benchmarks.pdf>.

Dewey, John, and Reginald D. Archambault. 1964. *John Dewey on Education: Selected Writings.* New York: Modern Library.

DFID (Department of International Development, UK). (nd). At <dfid.gov.uk>.

Dick, Bob. 2009. "Action Research Literature 2006–2008: Themes and Trends." *Action Research* 7, 4.

_____. 2007. "Action Research as an Enhancement of Natural Problem Solving." *International Journal of Action Research* 3, 1/2.

_____. 2006. "Action Research Literature: 2004–2006." *Action Research* 4, 4.

_____. 2004. "Action Research Literature: Themes and Trends." *Action Research* 2(4): 425–44.

Earl, Sarah, Fred Carden, and Terry Smutylo. 2001. *Outcome Mapping: Building Learning and Reflection into Development Programs.* Ottawa, ON: International Development Research Centre. At <idrc.ca>.

Edelman, Marc. 2001. "Social Movements: Changing Paradigms and Forms of Politics." *Annual Review of Anthropology* 30: 285–317.

Egbert, Marcia, and Susan Hoechstetter. 2007. "Evaluating Non-Profit Advocacy Simply: An Oxymoron?" *The Evaluation Exchange* 13.

Elliot, Charles. 1999. *Locating the Energy for Change: An Introduction to Appreciative Inquiry.* Winnipeg, MB: International Institute for Sustainable Development.

Evaluation Exchange. 2007. "Special Issue on Evaluating Advocacy and Policy Change." XIII 1. At <hfrp.org/evaluation>.

Fals Borda, Orlando. 2006. "The North-South Convergence: A 30 Year First Person Assessment of PAR." *Action Research* 4, 3.

Fals-Borda, Orlando, and Luis E. Mora-Osejo. 2003. "Context and Diffusion of Knowledge: A Critique of Eurocentrism." *Action Research* 1, 1.

Finn, Ed. 2010 (February). "Help Victims, Yes, But Better to Stop Their Victimization." *CCPA Monitor.* Ottawa, ON: Canadian Centre for Policy Alternatives.

Frampton, Caelie, Gary Kinsman, A.K. Thompson and Kate Tilliczek (eds.). 2006. "Social Movements/Social Research: Towards Political Activist Ethnography." In *Sociology for Changing the World: Social Movements/Social Research.* Halifax: Fernwood Publishing.

Freeman, Melissa (ed.). 2010. "Critical Social Theory and Evaluation Practice." *New Directions for Evaluation* 127, Fall.

Freire, Paolo. 1970. *Pedagogy of the Oppressed.* New York: Seabury Press.

Friedman, Thomas L. 2005. *The World Is Flat.* New York: Farrar, Strauss & Giroux.

Fukuda-Parr, Sakiko, and David Stewart. 2009. "Unequal Development in the 1990s: Growing Gaps in Human Capabilities." In Sudhir Anand, Paul Segal and Joseph Stiglitz (eds.), *Debates in the Measurement of Global Poverty.* Oxford University Press.

Galbraith, John Kenneth. 1993. *A Short History of Financial Euphoria.* New York: Penguin.

George, Susan. 1997. "How to Win the War of Ideas: Lessons from the Gramscian Right." *Dissent* 47–53.

Gergen, Kenneth. J. 2009. *An Invitation to Social Construction* (second edition). Thousand Oaks, CA: Sage.

Gergen, Kenneth. J., and Mary M. Gergen. 2008. "Social Construction and Research as Action." In Peter Reason and Hilary Bradbury (eds.), *The Sage Handbook of Action Research: Participative Inquiry and Practice*. Thousand Oaks, CA: Sage.

Gibb, Nancy. 2009. "In Defense of the Recession Blame Bame." *Time Magazine*, February 12.

Gienapp, Anne, Jane Reisman, and Sarah Stachowiak. 2009 (August). *Getting Started: A Self-Directed Guide to Outcome Map Development*. Prepared for the Annie E. Casey Foundation by Organizational Research Services. Seattle. At <organizational-researchcom>.

Gill, Carol J. 1994. "Questioning Continuum." In Barrett Shaw (ed.), *The Ragged Edge: The Disability Experience from the Pages of the First Fifteen Years of the Disability Rag*. Louisville, KY: Advocado Press.

Gramsci, Antonio. 1976. *Selections from the Prison Notebooks* (Edited and translated by Quintin Hoare and Geoffrey Nowell Smith). New York: International Publishers.

Greene, Jennifer C. 2010a. "Serving the Public Good.: *Evaluation and Program Planning* 33(2): 197–200.

_____. 2010b (September). "Snapshots of Integrated Analyses in Mixed Methods Evaluation." Presentation at the National Capital Chapter, Canadian Evaluation Society. Ottawa, ON.

_____. 2007. *Mixed Methods in Social Inquiry*. Thousand Oaks, CA: Sage.

_____. 2001. "Evaluation Extrapolations." *American Journal of Evaluation* 22(3): 397–402.

Greenwood, Davydd. 2007. "Pragmatic Action Research." *International Journal of Action Research* 3, 1/2.

Greenwood, Davydd, and Morten Levin. 2007. *Introduction to Action Research: Social Research for Social Change* (second edition). London: Sage.

Guijt, Irene. 2008. *Seeking Surprises: Rethinking Monitoring for Collective Learning in Rural Resource Management*. Wageningen, Netherlands: University of Wageningen.

Gustavsen, Bjorn. 2007. "Research Responses to Practical Challenges: What Can Action Research Contribute?" *International Journal of Action Research* 3 1/2.

Guthrie, Kendall, Justin Louie, Tom David, and Catherine Crystal Foster. 2005 (October). "The Challenge of Assessing Policy and Advocacy Activities: Strategies for a Prospective Evaluation Approach." A study conducted for the California Endowment. At <calendow.org>.

Hall, Budd. 1992 (December). "From Margins To Center? The Development and Purpose of Participatory Research." *The American Sociologist* 23, 4: 15–28.

Haluza-Delay, Randolph. 2003. "Community-Based Research, Movement Intellectuals and the 'Knowledge Council.'" *Canadian Review of Social Policy* 52 (Fall/Winter).

Harvard Family Research Project. 2007. *Evaluation Exchange 2007: A Periodical on Emerging Strategies in Evaluation*. Vol. 13 (1). Cambridge: MA: Harvard School of Education.

Held, David, Anthony McGrew, David Goldblatt, and Jonatho Perraton. 1999. *Global Transformations: Politics, Economics and Culture*. Stanford, CA: Stanford University Press.

Henry, Gary T., and Melvin M. Mark. 2003. "Beyond Use: Understanding

Evaluation's Influence on Attitudes and Actions." *American Journal of Evaluation* 24, 3: 293–314.

Herman E. Daly, and John B. Cobb, Jr. 1989. *For the Common Good: Redirecting the Economy Toward Community, and Environment and a Sustainable Future.* Boston: Beacon Press.

Hodgson, Dorothy L., and Ethel Brooks. 2007. "Introduction: Activisms." *Women's Studies Quarterly* 35/3&4 (fall/winter): 14–25.

Horton, Myles, and Paulo Freire. 1990. *We Make the Road by Walking: Conversations on Education and Social Change.* Philadelphia, PA: Temple University Press.

House, Ernest S., and Kenneth R. Howe. 1999. *Values in Evaluation and Social Research.* Thousand Oaks, CA: Sage.

Innovation Network, Inc. 2010 (January). "Advocacy Evaluation Update." Newsletter #8. At <innonet.org>.

_____. 2008 (September). "Speaking for Themselves: Advocates' Perspectives on Evaluation." A study commissioned by the A.E. Casey Foundation and the Atlantic Philanthropies. At <innonet.org>.

_____. nd. "Pathfinder: A Practical Guide to Advocacy Evaluation." Advocates Edition. At <innonet.org/advocacy>.

International Forum on Globalization (IFG). 1996. *IFG News* 1 (Fall).

International Labour Organization (ILO). 2008. "World of Work Report 2008." At <ilo.org/global/About_the_ILO/Media_and_public_information/Press_releases/lang--en/WCMS_099377/index.htm>.

JASS. 2006. "Making Change Happen: Citizen Engagement and Global Economic Power." Washington DC: Just Associates. At <justassociates.org>.

Johansson, Anders W., and Erik Lindhult. 2008. "Emancipation or Workability: Critical vs. Pragmatic Scientific Orientation in Action Research." *Action Research* 6, 1.

Just Associates. nd. "What is Success? Measuring and Evaluating the Impact of Social Justice Advocacy and Citizen Organizing Strategies." At <justassociates.org>.

Kellogg Foundation. 2007. "Designing Initiative Evaluation: A Systems-oriented Framework for Evaluating Social Shange Sfforts." Battle Creek, MI. At <wkkf.org>.

Kelly, Linda. 2002. "International Advocacy: Measuring Performance and Effectiveness." Paper presented at the 2002 Australasian Evaluation Society International Conference, Wollongong, Australia.

Keynes, John Maynard. 1926. *The End of Laissez-faire.* London: Hogarth.

Kirkhart, Karen. 2000. "Reconceptualizing Evaluation Use: Understanding Evaluation's Influence on Attitudes and Actions." *New Directions for Evaluation* 88.

Klein, Naomi. 2007. *The Shock Doctrine: The Rise of Disaster Capitalism.* New York: Metropolitan Books.

Klugman, Barbara. 2010 (August). "Evaluating Social Justice Advocacy: A Values Based Approach." At <www.evaluationinnovation.org>.

Korten, David. 2009. "Beyond Bailouts, Let's Put Life Ahead of Money." *Yes!* 48.

_____. 1996. *When Corporations Rule the World.* West Hartford, CT: Kumarian Press.

Kozul-Wright, R., and P. Rayment. 2004. *Globalization Reloaded: An UNCTAD Perspective.* Discussion Paper 167. New York: United Nations.

Kuhn, Thomas 1970. *The Structure of Scientific Revolutions* (second edition). Chicago: University of Chicago Press.

Kurtz, Cynthia F., and Donald J. Snowdon. 2003. "The New Dynamics of Strategy: Sense-Making in a Complex and Complicated World." *IBM Systems Journal* 42, 3.

La Rocca, Sam. 2004. "Making a Difference: Factors That Influence Participation in Grassroots Environmental Activism in Australia." Honours essay, Australian School of Environmental Studies, Griffith University. At <thechangeagency.com>.

Labonte, Ronald, and Joan Feather. 1996. *Handbook on Using Stories in Health Promotion Practice*. Ottawa, ON: Health Canada.

Laraia, Barbara A., Janice Dodds, and Eugenia Eng. 2003. "A Framework for Assessing the Effectiveness of Anti-Hunger Advocacy Organizations." *Health Education and Behavior* 30, 6.

Lempert, Ted. 2009 (February). "An Advocate's Perspective: Ten Considerations for Effective Advocacy Evaluation." At <organizationalresearch.com>. Also available at <innonet.org>.

Lenin, V.I. 1961. "What Is To Be Done? Burning Questions of Our Movement." In *Collected Works, Volume 5*. Moscow: Foreign Languages Publishing House.

Ludema, James D., David L. Cooperrider and Frank J. Barrett. 2001. "Appreciative Inquiry: The Power of the Unconditional Positive Question." In Peter Reason and Hilary Bradbury (eds.), *Handbook of Action Research*. London: Sage.

Lukács, Georg. 1971. "Reification and the Consciousness of the Proletariat." In *History and Class Consciousness*. Merlin Press. At <marxists.org/archive/lukacs/works/history/hcc05.htm>.

Mann, Michael. 1977. *Consciousness and Action Among the Western Working Class*. London: MacMillan.

Mark, Melvin M., and Gary T. Henry. 2004. "The Mechanisms and Outcomes of Evaluation Influence." *Evaluation* 10.

Martin, Paul. 1999. Quoted in *Globe and Mail* editorial, "In Praise of Regulation for the Market's Sake." June 9.

Martinez, Mark A. 2009. *The Myth of the Free Market: The Role of the State in a Capitalist Economy*. Sterling, VA: Kumarian Press.

Marx, Karl. 1845. "Theses on Feuerbach." In Karl Marx and Frederick Frederick (eds.), [1977] *Karl Marx and Frederick Engels: Selected Works in Three Volumes. Volume One*. Moscow: Progress Publishers.

_____. 1852. *The Eighteenth Brumaire of Louis Napoleon*. At <marxists.org/archive/marx/works/1852/18th-brumaire/ch01.htm>.

Marx, Karl, and Frederick Engels. 2005. "Manifesto of the Communist Party." In Phil Gasper (ed.), *Manifesto of the Communist Party: A Road Map to History's Most Important Political Document*. Chicago: Haymarket Books.

Masers, Barbara. 2009 (October). "Evaluating Policy Change and Advocacy: The Funder's Perspective." At <innonet.org>.

Masson, Richard, and Bryan Remillard. 1996. *Alberta's New Oil Sands Royalty System*. Edmonton AB: Alberta Department of Energy.

Mawdsley, J., J. Mikhareva, and J. Tennison. 2005. *The Oil Sands of Canada: The World Wakes Up: First to Peak Oil, Second to the Oil Sands of Canada*. Calgary AB: Raymond James Ltd.

Max-Neef, Manfred. 1997 (June). "On Human Economics." Keynote address at

Convergence: The World Congresses on Action Research, Action Learning and Process Management and Participatory Action-Research. Cartagena, Colombia.

Mayne, John. 2007. "Contribution Analysis: An Approach to Exploring Cause and Effect." ILAC (Institutional Learning and Change) Brief. <www.outcome-mapping.ca/download.php?file=/resource/files/csette_en_OLAC_Brief16_Contribution_Analysis.pfd>.

McGuigan, Claire. 2003. "*Advocacy Impact Assessment: A Literature Review.*" Save the Children, UK.

McMichael, Philip. 2010. "Changing the Subject of Development." In Philip McMichael (ed.), *Contesting Development: Critical Struggles for Social Change.* New York: Routledge.

McNally, David. 2002. *Another World Is Possible: Globalization and Anti-Capitalism.* Winnipeg, MB: Arbeiter Ring Publishing,

Menzies, Heather. 2005. *No Time: Stress and the Crisis of Modern Life.* Vancouver, BC: Douglas and McIntyre.

Miller, Carol. 2004 (May). "Measuring Policy Change: Assessing the Impact of Advocacy and Influencing Work." Unpublished report. C. Miller, Independent Consultant for One World Action.

Miller, Valerie. 1994. *NGO And Grassroots Policy Influence: What Is Success?* Washington DC: Institute for Development Research and Just Associates.

Mitchell, Robert, Brad Anderson, Marty Kaga, and Stephen Eliot. 1998. *Alberta's Oil Sands: Update on the Generic Royalty Regime.* Edmonton, AB: Alberta Department of Energy.

Monaco, Kay. 2007. "A Conversation with Kay Monaco." *The Evaluation Exchange* Harvard Family Research Project, 13, 1.

Moyer, Bill, with Joann McAllister, Mary Lou Finley, and Steven Soifer. 2001. *Doing Democracy: The MAP Model for Organizing Social Movements.* Gabriola Island, BC: New Society Publishers.

New Internationalist. 2009. "Special Issue on Climate Justice." January/February.

Nikiforuk, Andrew. 2008. *Tar Sands: Dirty Oil and the Future of a Continent.* Vancouver: David Suzuki Foundation-Greystone Books.

Oxfam America. 2007. "Ethiopia: Starbucks Campaign (Anatomy of a Win)" At <oxfam.org/en/development/ethiopia-starbucks-campaign-anatomy-win> November.

_____. 2004. "US Plans to Rejoin International Coffee Organization." At <globalex-change.org/campaigns/fair-trade/coffee/2528.html> September 16.

_____. 2002. "Mugged: Poverty in Your Coffee Cup." At <oxfamamerica.org/publications/mugged-poverty-in-your-coffee-cup> September 10.

Oxfam Canada. 2007. "Oxfam Celebrates Win-Win outcome on Ethiopian Coffee Farmers Campaign." At <oxfam.ca/news-and-publications/pressroom/press-releases/oxfam-celebrates-win-win-outcome-on-ethiopian-coffee-farmers-campaign> June 21.

_____. 2006a. "Oxfam Calls on Starbucks to Stop Bullying the Poor." At <oxfam.ca/news-and-publications/pressroom/press-releases/oxfam-calls-starbucks-stop-bullying-poor> November 3.

_____. 2006b. "Canadian Activists Target Starbucks on Rights of Ethiopian Famers:

Demonstrations in St. John's, Halifax, Ottawa and Edmonton." At <oxfam. ca/news-and-publications/pressroom/press-releases/canadian-activists-target-starbucks-rights-ethiopian-> December 15.

_____. 2006c. "Oxfam Canada's Campaigning Cup: Is it Half-empty or Half-full." Internal document of Oxfam Canada. February.

Panich, Leo. 1998. "Where the Left Began." *Globe and Mail* May 2.

Patel, Raj. 2009a. *The Value of Nothing: Why Everything Costs So Much More Than We Think.* Toronto, ON: HarperCollins.

_____. 2009b. "The Value of Nothing." Video posted on 11/11/2009. At <rajpatel.org>.

Patton, Michael Quinn. 2010. *Developmental Evaluation: Applying Complexity Concepts to Enhance Innovation and Use.* New York: Guilford.

_____. 2009 (January 20) "Developmental Evaluation: Evaluating under Conditions of Complexity." At <calendow.org/uploadedFiles/Evaluation/Patton%20 Developmental%20Evaluation.pdf? n=8316>.

_____. 2008 (March). "Advocacy Impact Evaluation." *Journal of Multidisciplinary Evaluation* 5, 9. At <plexusinstitute.org/edgeware>.

_____. 2003. "Inquiry into Appreciative Evaluation." In Hallie Preskill and Anne T. Coghlan (eds.), *Using Appreciative Inquiry in Evaluation: New Directions for Evaluation.* (Special Issue), 100. San Francisco: Jossey-Bass.

_____. 2002. *Qualitative Research and Evaluation Methods* (third edition). Thousand Oaks, CA: Sage.

Phelps, Renata, and Stewart Hase. 2002. "Complexity and Action Research: Exploring the Theoretical and Methodological Connections." *Educational Action Research* 10, 3.

Pigeon, Marc-Andre. 2003. *Tax Incentives and Expenditures Offered to the Oil Sands Industry.* Ottawa ON: Parliamentary Research Branch.

Polanyi, Karl. 1944. *The Great Transformation.* Toronto: Rinehart.

Preskill, Hallie, and Anne T. Coghlan (eds.). 2003. *Using Appreciative Inquiry in Evaluation: New Directions for Evaluation* (Special Issue), 100. San Francisco: Jossey-Bass.

Preskill, Hallie, and Tessie Tzavaras Catsambas. 2006. *Reframing Evaluation Through Appreciative Inquiry.* Thousand Oaks, CA: Sage.

Przeworski, Adam, et al. 1995. *Sustainable Democracy.* Cambridge: Cambridge University Press.

Putnam, Robert. 2000. *Bowling Alone: The Collapse and Revival of American Community.* New York: Simon and Schuster.

Pyrch, Timothy. 1998. "Introduction to the Action Research Family." *Studies in Cultures, Organizations & Societies* 4, 2: v–x.

Radford, Mike. 2007. "Action Research and the Challenge of Complexity." *Cambridge Journal of Education* 37, 2.

Ramalingam, Ben, and Harry Jones with Reba Toussaint and John Young 2008. *Exploring the Science of Complexity: Ideas and Implications for Development and Humanitarian Efforts.* Working Paper 285 (Second Edition). London: Overseas Development Institute (ODI).

Ranghelli, Lisa. 2009. "Measuring the Impacts of Advocacy and Community Organizing: Application of a Methodology and Initial Findings." *Foundation Review* 1, 3.

Ransom, David. 2009. "The Age of Possibility." *New Internationalist* 421.

Raynor, Jared. 2009 (January 20). "Evaluating Organizational Advocacy Capacity:

A Short-Term Measure of Success." At <calendow.org/uploadedFiles/ Evaluation/Raynor%20Advocacy%20Capacity.pdf>.

Raynor, Jared, Peter York, and Chao-Chee Sim. 2009 (January). "What Makes an Effective Advocacy Organization: A Framework for Determining Advocacy Capacity?" The California Endowment. At <calendow.org>.

Reason, Peter, and Hilary Bradbury. 2007. "Editorial." *Action Research* 5, 4.

_____ (eds.). 2006. *Handbook of Action Research* (second edition). London: Sage.

_____ (eds.). 2001. *Handbook of Action Research: Participative Inquiry and Practice.* London: Sage.

Reilly, Molly. 2007 (February). "An Agenda for Change in the USA: Insights From a Conversation about Assessing Social Change in Washington DC." At <justassociates.org>.

Reisman, Jane, Anne Gienapp, and Sarah Stachowiak. 2007. "A Guide to Measuring Advocacy And Policy." Prepared for the Annie E. Casey Foundation by Organizational Research Services. At <organizationalresearch.com> and <aecf.org>.

Rihani, Samir. 2002. *Complexity Systems Theory and Development Practice: Understanding Non-Linear Realities.* London: Zed.

Ringsing, Bettina, and Cees Leeuwis. 2008. "Learning About Advocacy: A Case Study of Challenges, Everyday Practices and Tensions." *Evaluation* 14, 4.

Robinson-Easley, Christopher Ann. 1998. "The Role of Appreciative Inquiry in the Fight to Save our Youth." Unpublished doctoral dissertation, Benedictine University. Naperville, Illinois.

Rose, Chris (2005). *How to Win Campaigns: 100 Steps to Success.* London: Earthscan.

Rosenhead, Jonathan. 1998. *Complexity Theory and Management Practice.* Working paper LSEOR 9825, London School of Economics, Operational Research (ISBN:0 7530 12537).

Schaefer, Stephanie. 2007. "What Does Monitoring and Evaluation Look Like for Real-Life Advocates." *The Evaluation Exchange* XIII.

Schell, Jonathan. 2003. "The Other Superpower." *The Nation* April 14.

Shaw, Barrett (ed.). 1994. *The Ragged Edge: The Disability Experience from the Pages of the First Fifteen Years of the Disability Rag.* Louisville, KY: Advocado Press.

Shaw, Greg. 2008. "Commentary on the Case of Great Start and the Missing Child Outcomes." *American Journal of Evaluation* 29, 4 (December).

Skolits, Gary J., Jennifer Ann Murrow, and Erin Mehalic Burr. 2009. "Reconceptualizing Evaluator Roles." *American Journal of Evaluation* 30, 3.

Smith, Dorothy. 1986. "Institutional Ethnography: A Feminist Method." *Resources for Feminist Research* 15, 10.

Smith, George. 2006. "Political Activist as Ethnographer." In Caelie Frampton, Gary Kinsman, AK Thompson and Kate Tilliczek (eds.), *Sociology for Changing the World: Social Movements/Social Research.* Halifax: Fernwood Publishing.

Smith, Linda Tuhiwai. 1999. *Decolonizing Methodologies: Research and Indigenous Peoples.* London: Zed Books.

Snowden, David J., and Mary E. Boone. 2007. "A Leader's Framework For Decision Making." *Harvard Business Review* 85, 11

Soros, George. 1998. *The Crisis of Global Capitalism: Open Society Endangered.* New York: Public Affairs.

Stachowiak, Sarah. 2009. "Pathways For Change: Six Theories about How Policy Change Happens." Seattle, WA: Organizational Research Services. At <organizationalresearch.com/publications_and_resources.htm#pfc6tahpc>.

Stanford, Jim. 2008. *Economics for Everyone: A Short Guide to the Economics of Capitalism.* Halifax and Winnipeg: Fernwood Publishing.

Stephens, Michael. 2009. "Toward Good Practice in Public Engagement: A Participatory Evaluation Guide for CSOs." Ottawa: Canadian Council for International Co-operation. At <ccic.ca>.

Stienstra, Deborah, and Aileen Wight-Felskey. 2003. *Making Equality: History of Advocacy and Persons With Disabilities in Canada.* Concord, ON: Captus Press.

Stiglitz, Joseph. 2010. "The Non-Existent Hand. *London Review of Books* 32: 17–18.

Strega, Susan. 2005. "The View from the Post-Structural Margins: Epistemology and Methodology Reconsidered." In Leslie Brown and Susan Strega (eds.), *Research as Resistance: Critical, Indigenous, and Anti-Oppressive Approaches.* Toronto, ON: Canadian Scholars' Press.

Stuart, Ricky, and Sandy McAlpine. 2003. "Wake Up and Smell the Coffee." *Globe and Mail,* June 12. At <evalu8.org/staticpage?page=review&siteid=2523>.

Torjman, Sherri. 1999. "Are Outcomes the Best Outcome?" Ottawa, Caledon Institute of Social Policy. At <caledoninst.org>.

Touraine, Alain. 1971. *The May Movement; Revolt and Reform: May 1968—The Student Rebellion and Workers' Strikes—The Birth of a Social Movement.* Translated by Leonard F.X. Mayhew. New York: Random House.

United Nations (UN). 2010. "Rethinking Poverty." *UN Report on the World Social Situation.* Division for Social Policy and Development of the Department of Economic and Social Affairs. At <un.org/esa/socdev/rwss/2010.html>.

_____. 2009. "Millennium Development Goals Report." At <un.org/millenniumgoals/>.

United Nations Development Programme (UNDP). 2007/2008. *Human Development Report.* New York: Palgrave/Macmillan.

_____ 1999. *Human Development Report.* Cary, NC: Oxford University Press.

_____. 1997. *Human Development Report 1997.* At <undp.org>.

USAID Advocacy Framework. n.d. "Appendix 2. Supporting Civic Advocacy: Strategic Approaches For Donor-Supported Civic Advocacy Programs." (Draft version) USAID Office of Democracy and Governance. At <usaid.gov>.

Veneklasen, Lisa, and Valerie Miller. 2002. "The Advocacy Debate: Changing Policy, Changing People." International Institute for Education and Development. *PLA Notes* 43: 13.

Via Campesina. 2009. At <viacampesina.org/main_en/>.

Victor, Peter A. 2008. *Managing Without Growth: Slower By Design, Not Disaster.* Cheltenham, UK and Northampton, MA: Edward Elgar.

Wade, Cheryl Marie. 1994. "Disability Culture Rap." In Barrett Shaw (ed.), *The Ragged Edge: The Disability Experience from the Pages of the First Fifteen Years of the Disability Rag.* Louisville, KY: Advocado Press.

Westley, Frances, Brenda Zimmerman, and Michael Quinn Patton. 2006. *Getting to Maybe: How the World Is Changed.* Toronto, ON: Random House.

Whalen, Justin. 2008. "Advocacy Evaluation: Review and Opportunities." At <thechangeagency.org>.

_____. 2006 (June). "Assessing Advocacy." At <thechangeagency.org>.

Whitmore, Elizabeth, and Maureen G. Wilson 2005. "Popular Resistance to Global Corporate Rule: The Role of Social Work." In Iain Ferguson, Michael Lavalette and Elizabeth Whitmore, Elizabeth (eds.), *Globalisation, Global Justice and Social Work*. New York: Routledge.

Wiebe, Nettie. 1998. "Citizenship: Our Social Commitment." Ottawa, Opening address to *Citizens' Action Social Watch National Forum* December.

Wilson, Maureen G., and Iris Prado Hernández. 2007. "The Liberatory Tradition in Nicaraguan Social Work." In Iain Ferguson and Michael Lavalette (eds.), *Radical Social Work in an Era of Globalisation*. Birmingham, UK: Venture Press.

Wilson, Maureen G., and Elizabeth Whitmore. 2000. *Seeds of Fire: International Development in an Era of Globalism*. Co-published by Halifax, NS: Fernwood Publishing and Ottawa: Canaidna Consortium for International Social Development, and New York: Apex

Wilson, Shawn. 2008. *Research as Ceremony: Indigenous Research methods*. Halifax, NS: Fernwood Publishing.

Wilson-Grau, Ricardo, and Martha Nuñez. 2007. "Evaluating International Social Change Networks: A Conceptual Framework for a Participatory Approach." *Development in Practice* 17.

Woodhill, Jim. 2009 (December). "Introduction." In Seerp Wigboldus and Mirjam Schaap (eds.), *Innovation Dialogue: Being Strategic in the Face of Complexity*. Conference report. Wageningen, The Netherlands: Wageningen UR Centre for Development Innovation. At <cdi.wur.nl/UK/>.

_____. 2007. "M&E as Learning: Rethinking the Dominant Paradigm." In Jan de Graaf, John Camerson, Samran Sombatpanit, Christian Pieri and Jom Woodhill (eds.). *Monitoring and Evaluation of Social Conservation and Watershed Development Projects*. Endfield, NH: Science Publishers.

World Bank Advocacy Framework. n.d. "Appendix 3: Community Empowerment and Social Inclusion (CESI) Module on Participatory Planning for Advocacy, Communication and Coalition Building." At <worldbank.org>.

Worth, Jess. 2009a. "Four Principles for Climate Justice." *New Internationalist* 419 (January/February).

_____. 2009b. "Can Climate Catastrophe Be Averted?" *The CCPA Monitor*. Ottawa, ON: Canadian Centre for Policy Alternatives.

Zandee, Danielle P., and David L. Cooperrider. 2008. "Appreciable Worlds, Inspired Inquiry." In Peter Reason and Hilary Bradbury (eds.), *The Sage Handbook of Action Research: Participative Inquiry and Practice*. Thousand Oaks, CA: Sage.

Zimmerman, Brenda. 2000. "A Complexity Science Primer: What is Complexity Science and Why Should I Learn About It?" At <plexusinstitute.com/edgeware>.

Websites

<www.actionhall.ca>
<www.caledonist.org>
<www.proudtobedisabled.com>
<www.ptf.org>

INDEX